PAPERCRAFTS

Papercrafts

100 fantastic paper projects, step-by-step

Angela A'Court & Marion Elliot,
with Paul Jackson

SMITHMARK

© Anness Publishing Limited

All our rights reserved. No part of this publication may be
reproduced, stored in a retrieval system, or transmitted in
any way or by any means, electronic, mechanical,
photocopying, recording or otherwise, without first obtaining
written permission of the copyright owner.

This edition published in 1994 by
SMITHMARK Publishing Inc.
16 East 32nd Street
New York
NY 10016

SMITHMARK books are available for bulk purchase for sales
promotion and premium use. For details write or call
the manager of special sales, SMITHMARK Publishers Inc.,
16 East 32nd Street, New York, NY 10016; (212) 532-6600.

Produced by Anness Publishing Ltd
1 Boundary Row
London SE1 8HP

ISBN 0-8317-6225-X

Printed and bound in Singapore

10 9 8 7 6 5 4 3 2 1

CONTENTS

Introduction   7

Decorative Papercrafts   9

Paper Projects   89

Index   128

INTRODUCTION

Paper is everywhere: our lives would be impossible without wrappings, letters, magazines, cards, packaging, leaflets, posters, newspapers and notepads. It is one of the most inexpensive and readily available of materials, yet it is commonly neglected as a craft, art and hobby medium. With know-how, imagination and enthusiasm, papercraft skills, origami techniques and papier-mâché artistry can transform this simple, functional and cost-effective material into fantastic gifts, wonderful shapes, delightful stationery and beautiful objects, such as toys, bags, jewellery and boxes.

Decorative Papercrafts

NATTY NAPKINS

Here is a very quick way to add your own style to ordinary napkins and add a sparkle to the tone of your meal! Even a squiggle, a dot, or a circle can transform the napkin. Try experimenting with different shapes, and perhaps give everybody their own design.

YOU WILL NEED
Plain coloured paper napkins
Pen
Gold and silver metallic pens

2 Then take a silver metallic pen with a medium nib and carefully trace over the pen lines.

1 For a Christmas feel use a plain red napkin and lightly mark out a holly leaf and berry sprig in pen.

3 For a Hallowe'en evening take a black napkin and draw gold stars and half moons with a gold pen.

■ TWO-TONE GIFTWRAP

Here is another way to make your own wrapping paper, this time using two layers of co-ordinating crêpe paper.

YOU WILL NEED
Crêpe paper in two contrasting colours
Glue

1 First work out how much paper you will need in order to cover the gift. Now cut a piece of paper to this size in each of your two chosen colours. Decide which colour will be on top and pleat it lengthwise.

2 Now cut circles out through all the layers along both sides of the pleat.

3 Open up the top paper and glue it onto the bottom. It is exciting to see how the colour of the bottom layer shows through. If you want a really elaborate design, add cut-out pieces in a further colour, leaving openings large enough to reveal the colours beneath. Now wrap your gift up in the two-tone dotty paper.

■ BAROQUE BAUBLES

We have used a polystyrene ball for this decoration. They can be found, in a range of sizes, in craft shops and are used for making dolls' heads.

YOU WILL NEED
Polystyrene ball
Gouache paint
Gold doily
Glue
Brass paper fastener
Gold thread

1 First of all, paint the bauble with some gouache in a suitable colour.

2 When the paint has dried, cut out pieces from a doily. Decide how they are to be arranged on the bauble and glue them into position.

3 Cut out a further motif from the doily and take a brass paper fastener and push it through the centre. Now push this into the top of the ball.

4 Taking some gold thread, wrap it around the brass fastener so that it is ready to be hung on the Christmas tree.

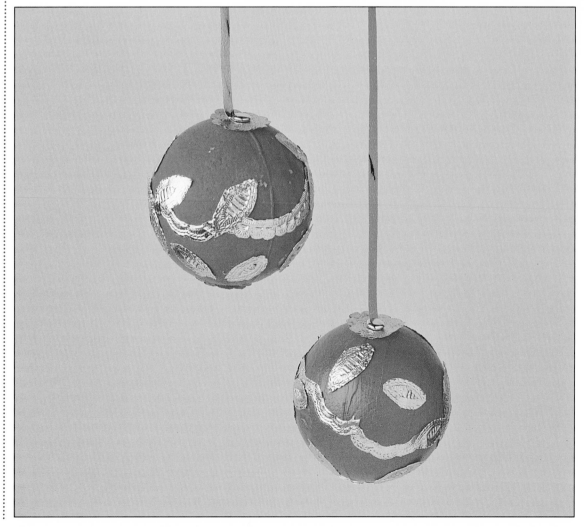

ORIENTAL FAN

Here is an easy way to make a beautiful fan to cool yourself on a hot summer's day. This fan is loosely designed on a Japanese fan and so we have made it with Japanese rice paper.

YOU WILL NEED
Thin card
Craft knife
Glue
Double-sided tape
Rice paper or tissue paper

1 Cut out an oval piece of thin card. Make sure that the card is not too thick so that it is flexible for fanning. Cut out the bottom area of the fan with a craft knife.

2 Next cut thin strips of card and lining them up at the base, stick them on both sides of the fan so that they follow the cut out lines.

3 To make the handle, cut out two strips of thicker card measuring 14 × 1½ cm (5½ × ½ in). Taper the ends and stick double-sided tape onto both pieces. Attach them to either side of the base part of the fan.

4 Now cover the fan in rice paper by gluing round the edge and along the struts. We have used a different colour paper on either side for variety. If you cannot find rice paper, use tissue paper instead. Trim the edges with scissors.

5 Cover the handle by wrapping it with a long strip of rice paper and gluing it at the bottom.

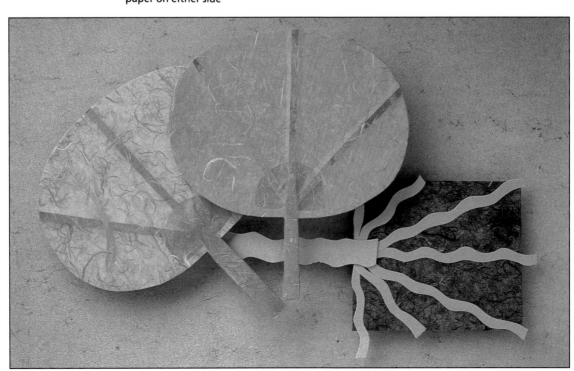

WELL-DRESSED NAPKIN

Here is a quick and simple way to dress up a napkin using coloured card. You can make the holder in contrasting or a toning coloured card to suit the setting.

YOU WILL NEED
Paper napkins
Thin card in two contrasting colours
Glue

1 First cut a square of card to the same size as the folded napkin.

2 Fold the card diagonally with the front fold halfway up. Cut a triangle in contrasting coloured card slightly smaller than the front triangle. Cut out a zigzag edge along two sides.

3 Now fold the napkin in half and place it into the napkin holder. Why not experiment with different designs on the front, or leave it plain and glue on a cut out motif from a magazine.

GIFT BOX

Here is an easy and stylish way to present an awkwardly-shaped gift. It also makes a lovely box to use afterwards to keep things in.

YOU WILL NEED
Empty shoe box with lid
Patterned and plain wrapping paper
Glue
Tissue paper

1 Wrap the outside of the box in the patterned paper.

2 Now line the inside of the box with plain paper.

3 Cover the lid of the box on the top and inside in the plain paper. Take some tissue paper in a co-ordinating colour, softly scrunch it up and arrange it in the bottom of the box. Place the gift inside and put the lid on.

4 As a further decoration, enhance the top by attaching paper strips cut from the patterned paper to suggest ribbons.

CLASSIC LINES

If you want to write a letter in a hurry, but still want it to be stylish, here are a couple of quick ways to make some beautiful writing paper. You will need some lightly coloured wrapping paper in a classical design.

YOU WILL NEED
Pale wrapping paper
Tracing paper
Glue
Sheet of white paper

1 Cut out a rectangle of wrapping paper to the size of writing paper, and cut a piece of tracing paper to the same size. Stick the tracing paper on top of the wrapping paper, smoothing out any bubbles. Use a black felt-tip pen to write your letter so that it shows up clearly.

2 If you have a bit more time you could select one particular motif from the paper and cut this out.

3 Glue the motif to a sheet of white paper.

4 As before, glue a sheet of tracing paper on top to give an elegant double layer. You could make a collection of writing paper by cutting out different motifs from one sheet of wrapping paper.

PAINT AND PAPER

Have fun turning an ordinary piece of black paper into bright and jazzy wrapping paper. You could of course vary the colour of the paper and paints.

YOU WILL NEED
Plain paper
Paints

2 Add more colours as you wish until the paper is brightly decorated.

1 Take a piece of black paper large enough to cover your present. Now choose the paint colours you are going to use. This example uses fuchsia pink, orange and gold paints to contrast with the black background. After preparing the paint on a saucer, decorate the paper with random 'blobs', working with one colour at a time.

3 For a more regular painted pattern, the present can be wrapped first and then, following the shape of the gift, painted with wavy lines.

TWELFTH KNIGHT

Whether entertaining the Knights of the Round Table or just arranging a boys' party, these heraldic place mats will certainly set the tone.

YOU WILL NEED
Silver, purple and orange card
Glue

2 Cut out eight wavy lines in orange card and five dots in purple card. Using the template, scaled to the size required, draw and cut out the fleur-de-lys shape.

1 Place mat
■ To make this heraldic place mat, trace out a shield shape onto silver card and cut it out. It should have a width and length of about 25 cm (10 in). Cut six strips of purple card measuring 2 × 27 cm (¾ × 11 in). Glue and place two strips to form a cross on the shield and trim at the edges.

3 Following the design in the photograph, arrange all the shapes onto your card and glue them into place one by one.

4 Napkin holder
■ Take a piece of purple card 22 × 5 cm (9 × 2 in). Join the short ends together and glue. Cut out a small silver shield in card and an orange fleur-de-lys. Glue together and then glue onto the napkin holder.

5 Name place card
■ To complete the heraldic theme, make up a name place. Cut a piece of silver card 9 × 10 cm (3½ × 4 in) and fold it lengthways down the centre. Cut out a smaller fleur-de-lys shape 4 cm (1½ in) high in purple card and glue it onto the silver card. Add the orange band.

ELEGANT ENVELOPES

Finding the right size and style of envelope to match your home-made stationery can be a problem, so why not make your own?

YOU WILL NEED
Coloured card
Glue
Contrasting coloured card

1 Measure out the size that you require by placing your card onto a piece of coloured card. It must be twice as long plus 3 cm (1 in), and as wide plus 6 cm (2 in). For a pointed flap you will need an extra 10 cm (4 in) on the length.

2 Cut off the excess corners and then fold up the bottom and sides and stick them down.

3 Cut out a motif to stick on the back flap in a different colour. If the envelope has a pointed flap you might like to make this a contrasting colour by cutting out a triangle to the same size and gluing it to the back flap.

IT'S A CRACKER

Sometimes a gift has such an obvious shape that even when it has been wrapped up it is immediately recognizable. Here is a fun way to disguise the shape by dressing it up as a cracker.

YOU WILL NEED
Cardboard tube
Wrapping paper
Double-sided tape
Ribbon

1 Place your gift inside the cardboard tube and cut a piece of wrapping paper so that it extends about 10 cm (4 in) at either end. Roll the paper around and secure it with tape. For a really professional look double-sided tape should be used.

2 Now cut two lengths of ribbon and tie at each end of the tube. Trim the ribbon ends. For a more colourful effect you could use several colours of ribbon.

3 Holding the cracker in one hand, cut a zigzag design at the end and then turn around and repeat with the other end.

■ STENCILLING

Stencilling is a very popular craft and a huge variety of effects can be achieved. Stencilled patterns can be combined with other decorative techniques such as speckling or batik effects using wax crayons. Either a stencilling brush or a sponge can be used to apply the paint through the stencil; a brush will give a stippled effect, and a sponge a solid, denser result.

YOU WILL NEED
Stencilling card
Craft knife
Paper
Assortment of paints
Piece of sponge
Stencil brush

1 Draw a design onto the stencilling card and cut it out carefully using a craft knife.

2 Lay a piece of paper onto a flat surface and place the stencil on top over the intended position of the design. Mix the paint until it is quite sticky in consistency; take up a fair amount of paint using the sponge and carefully dab it over the pattern in the stencilling card. Take care not to let the paint become too thin as it will seep under the edges of the stencil, giving a blurred design.

3 To use a stencil brush, lay a sheet of paper down on a flat surface and place the stencil on top. Load the brush with fairly thick paint and press it gently over the stencil, covering the paper beneath. Again, make sure the paint is not too thin. Dab paint over the stencil so that a mottled effect is achieved.

RIBBON PLAITS AND CURLS

There are many different effects that can be achieved by mixing and matching coloured ribbons. They can be plaited or twisted and grouped into colours to cascade down a wrapped present.

YOU WILL NEED
Assortment of ribbons
Double-sided tape
Felt-tip pens
Gold metallic pen

1 One of the most straightforward ways to use ribbon is to curl it. This effect is achieved by pulling the ribbon through closed scissors to make it twist and fall into natural ringlets. Try doing this to different lengths and colours of ribbons and then attach a bunch of curls to your present.

2 Another effective way to use ribbon is to plait it, using at least three different colours. Tape the ribbon ends together and plait to the required length. Secure and cut the ribbon ends.

3 In this example a whole medley of ribbons in different colours and widths is plaited together in order to create a riot of colour. Tape and cut ribbon ends.

4 To give ribbon an individual look, decorate it by drawing a design taken from the wrapping paper with a felt-tip or metallic pen.

■ TAG TIME

Make your own gift tags for a personal touch as well as to save money. Used greetings cards can often be cut down and made into brand new gift tags. Another idea is to take a motif from the wrapping paper used to cover your present.

YOU WILL NEED
Wrapping paper or greetings cards
Glue
Thin card
Ribbon

1 When you have wrapped the present, cut out a suitable motif from the spare paper. Glue the motif onto some thin card in a co-ordinating colour.

2 Following the shape of the motif cut around the design so that the card forms a border.

3 Now punch a hole in the card with a scissor blade and thread a ribbon through the hole. Write a message on the tag and attach it to the present.

▪ STRAIGHT-SIDED BOX

This pretty box is made in two parts; each half can be in a different colour to create a contrast effect. It is assembled using a clever interlocking action.

YOU WILL NEED
Thin card in two different colours
Craft knife
Glue

1 Both halves are made in the same way. Scale up the template for the two halves of the box to the size required and transfer to the coloured card. Cut out the pieces with a craft knife. Fold in and glue the side tabs.

2 To assemble the box, interlock the two halves by first tucking each tongue beneath the shallow edge on all sides of the box. Push the halves together to close the box.

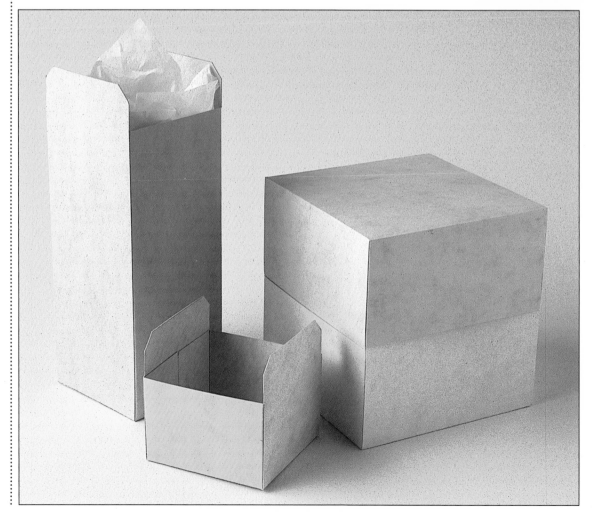

BATIK
EFFECTS

Lovely batik-like effects can be achieved on paper with wax crayons and thin paint. Designers' inks, which have very intense colours, can be used for striking results.

YOU WILL NEED
White and coloured paper
Wax crayons
Assorted poster or gouache paints, or designers' inks
Clear wax candle

1 Draw a design onto white paper with wax crayons, using either a single colour or a variety. Load a paint brush with thin paint or diluted ink and brush it over the wax. Two coats of paint can be applied to achieve a stronger colour layer where required.

2 To create a multi-coloured effect where the base colour of the paper will show through, use a clear wax candle to draw the design onto coloured paper. Paint over the wax marks with one colour and leave to dry. Next, make more wax marks and paint over the paper again with a second colour so that the second set of designs will take on the colour of the first layer of paint.

Every piece of writing paper will be different using this technique of tearing and gluing paper to create an abstract design.

YOU WILL NEED
Craft knife
Writing paper
Card in two contrasting colours
Glue

1 Using a craft knife, cut a small rectangle at the top of the writing paper, in the centre. Next, choose two pieces of different colour card just large enough to cover the opening, and tear one in half.

2 Glue one of the torn halves onto the other whole rectangle.

3 Glue this onto the back of the letter-head.

4 Instead of using a plain card, a favourite patterned wrapping paper can be put behind the opening. Different shaped openings can be cut for the effect you like. In this step some paper is glued on to card and then slotted in and glued so that it breaks up the top line of the paper.

5 Of course the plain and patterned papers can be mixed.

SPECKLING EFFECTS

Speckling produces a variety of results depending on how the paint is applied, and on how sharply the brush is shaken. Gentle taps produce fine marks, rather like freckles. More boisterous movements can produce a more startling effect.

YOU WILL NEED
A selection of papers
Assorted poster or gouache paints
Length of wood or other object to tap brush against
Nail brush
Stiff cardboard

1 Lay the sheet of paper to be speckled on a flat surface. Mix the paint to a fairly thin consistency and load a paint brush with it. Hold the length of wood over the paper and bring the brush down on the wood, tapping along its length over the paper to produce a speckled effect.

2 More than one colour of speckling can be applied; colours that tone in with the first layer of paint or even those which contrast sharply with it can look very effective. To obtain a fine spray of speckles dip a nail brush in thin paint and position it over the paper, holding it with the bristles uppermost. Pull a strip of cardboard over the bristles (taking care to pull it *towards* your body so that you do not splash yourself with paint), moving the brush around the paper to create an even coating of paint.

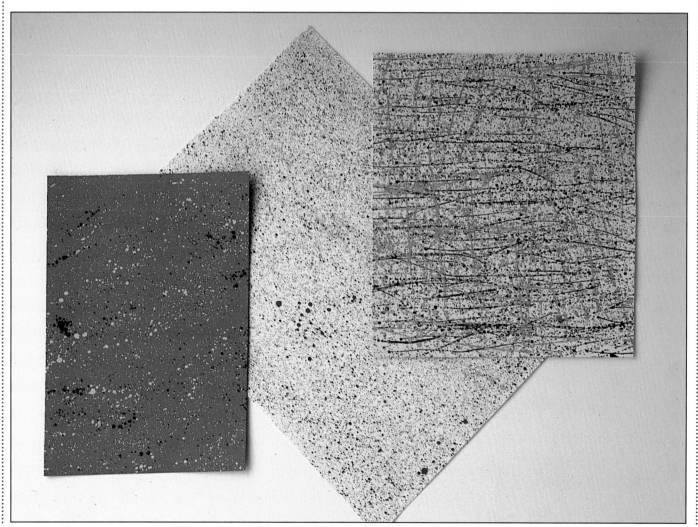

CURVY-EDGED BOX

This unusual box is almost as pretty in two halves as it is when assembled. To get the maximum effect choose two contrasting or complementary colours for the two halves so that the pattern of the curves stands out.

YOU WILL NEED
Thin card in two different colours
Craft knife
Glue

1 Scale up the template to the size required and transfer the pattern twice to a piece of card, once for each half of the box. Cut out the patterns using a craft knife, taking extra care around the curves. Both halves are made in the same way: fold and glue each tab beneath the semi-circles to form the sides.

2 Repeat the process with the other half, gluing each side firmly.

3 To assemble the box, interlock the two halves, making sure each semi-circle overlaps on the outside of the box.

QUILLS
AND COILS

Quilling is a traditional way of rolling strips of coloured paper and then squeezing them into different shapes; they are used here to decorate cards.

YOU WILL NEED
Coloured paper
Glue
Contrasting coloured card
Hole punch
Ribbon

1 To make up the individual quills, cut strips of coloured paper 7 × 25 cm (2¾ × 10 in). Starting with one end, roll the paper up.

2 When you have rolled it completely, let it uncoil slightly and glue the end to hold it.

3 Once the strip has been coiled and glued it can be shaped into one of the many traditional quill styles, such as the triangle, or the pear, or the scroll or the eye.

4 Take a piece of folded card in a good background colour and arrange the quills into a pattern. Punch a hole with a hole punch and thread a ribbon through to make an original and delightful miniature card or gift tag.

■ BOOKLET CARD

Just a small piece of wrapping paper from your gift is enough to make this booklet card or gift tag. Secure with embroidery thread to match.

YOU WILL NEED
White card
Wrapping paper
Glue
Ruler
Craft knife
Writing paper
Needle
Embroidery thread

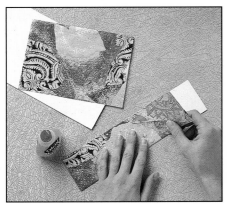

1 Take a piece of
■ white card 28 × 7
cm (11 × 2¾ in) and
cut out a piece of
wrapping paper the
same size. Glue this
paper onto the card.

2 On the reverse,
■ lightly score a line
at the centre using a
ruler and craft knife,
and fold in two to
make the outer card.

3 Then cut a piece
■ of white writing
paper so that it is
just smaller than the
card and fold this in
two.

4 With a needle
■ and some
embroidery thread
to match the
wrapping paper, sew
the two layers
together with one
stitch, and tie the
threads into a knot
to secure the
booklet.

THIS LITTLE PIGGY

Great for children's parties or for a more adult gathering, this piggy place setting will bring oinks of delight! Choose bright pink, or a pale pink for a Miss Piggy.

YOU WILL NEED
Circular plate
Pink, green and blue card
Glue
Craft knife
Felt-tip pen

1 Place mat
■ Using a plate as a template, mark and cut out a circle about 24 cm (10 in) in diameter in pink card, remembering to include two ear shapes.

2 Using green and
■ blue card, cut out and glue all the features of the face into position.

3 Then attach the
■ curly tail to the right-hand side in order to give the

finishing touch to your pig place mat.

4 Name place card
■ To make up the name card, take a piece of green card measuring 9 cm (3½ in) square. Draw a line down the centre and around the top

half of the pig's head and ears. Score along the head and ears only and then gently fold, and the pig's head will stand up.

5 Glue the piggy's
■ features as before onto a piece of pink card and then attach

the finished face on to the folded card. Add the curly tail.

6 Napkin holder
■ Take a strip of pink card measuring 22 × 5 cm (8½ × 2 in) and glue the ends together.

Before the glue has dried, slip a green curly tail card under the join and hold firmly until it is dry.

DECORATIVE PAPERCRAFTS

TIGER STRIPES AND HOPPING FROGS

Here are some ideas for making writing paper with an animal theme. You can use these ideas to design original writing paper, based on your favourite animal.

YOU WILL NEED
Orange, black, blue and green paper
Glue
Writing paper

1 To make a jungle theme take a piece of orange paper and cut out 'stripey' shapes from a piece of black paper.

2 Arrange the tiger stripes down one side of the paper and glue them into position.
   To add colour to a sheet of white writing paper you can also cut out an abstract squiggle and glue it onto the right hand side.

3 For a fishy theme cut out shapes of watery ripples and a swimming fish from blue paper and then stick them at the top and bottom of the page.

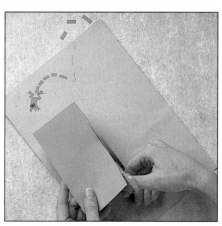

4 This hopping frog theme is made by cutting out a frog shape in green paper and fixing it to the top of the page. You will then need to cut out and glue small squares of green paper to represent its hop!

PAPER-MAKING

Paper-making is an ancient art form, practised for many centuries since the process was first discovered by the Chinese. It can be very satisfying to make your own paper. If you want to make paper of writing quality, dissolve two teaspoons of size powder in a pint of warm water and add it to your pulp. It is possible to produce many interesting effects in your paper. Small pieces of coloured paper can be added to the pulp to give a speckled effect; this can also be achieved by adding organic material such as tea leaves, seeds, hair, leaves and flower petals. It is also possible to colour and perfume your paper by adding waterproof ink or a few drops of scent to the pulp.

YOU WILL NEED
Waste paper
Blender or liquidizer
Fine sieve
Rectangular bowl
Kitchen cloths (one for each piece of paper to be made) or towelling
Newspaper
Paper-making frame (deckle and mould)
Two wooden boards

MAKING PULP

To make paper pulp, tear up waste paper into small pieces. The lighter the colour of waste paper used, the paler the result; newspaper will produce a greyish paper. Old computer printout paper is good. Place the torn paper in a bucket of warm water and let it soak overnight. To reduce the paper to a pulp, squeeze out as much water as possible, and place a small handful of the mushy paper into a blender or liquidizer, covering it with two parts of water. Blend the paper and water together for a few seconds at a time. Add more water if the pulp is too thick for the blender to rotate freely.

1 When you have pulped all the soaked paper, drain it through a fine sieve, and place three or four handfuls in the rectangular bowl. Cover the pulp with warm water. You will need roughly three parts of water to one part pulp.
   Before you start to make your paper, prepare a 'couching mound'. This is a small pile of wet material such as kitchen cloths or towelling, cut or folded to the same size as the frame and placed on top of a thick wedge of newspaper. The pulp is transferred from the mould onto this mound to dry.

2 Take your paper-making frame. The mesh-covered frame is called the mould, and the open frame is the deckle. Position the mould mesh-side up, and place the deckle on top of it.

3 Put the frame into the far end of the bowl, with the deckle facing you.

4 Next, submerge the frame in the pulp.

5 Pull the frame gently towards you, while holding on to keep it tightly closed and completely submerged. Lift the frame from the bowl, keeping it horizontal. Let the frame rest on the side of the bowl for a minute to drain, and then remove the deckle.

6 Stand the mould on its short side and lower it onto the couching mound, pressing it down firmly. Then lift the bottom edge off the couching cloth, and remove the frame. The pulp will stick to the cloth. Cover the pulp with an opened-out kitchen cloth, and continue couching sheets of paper, covering each new piece with another kitchen cloth.

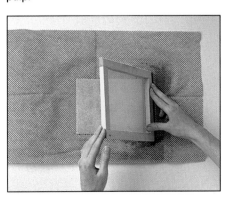

7 When you have used all the pulp, or feel that you have made enough paper, cover the last piece with a kitchen cloth, and transfer the pile of cloths containing your paper on its couching mound and pile of newspaper onto one of the wooden boards. The board should be placed on a surface that is easy to mop dry as a great deal of water will come out of the paper.

Place the second board on top of the pile, and then stand or lean heavily on it to press the paper flat. Press on the paper for a couple of minutes.

Remove the pile of cloths from the newspaper, then gently lift the top cloth, uncovering the last piece of paper that you made, and lay it out, still on its cloth, on a flat surface to dry. Do the same with every piece of paper. The sheets may take two days to dry properly. To remove the paper from its drying cloth, slip a blunt knife under its edge and gently separate the two.

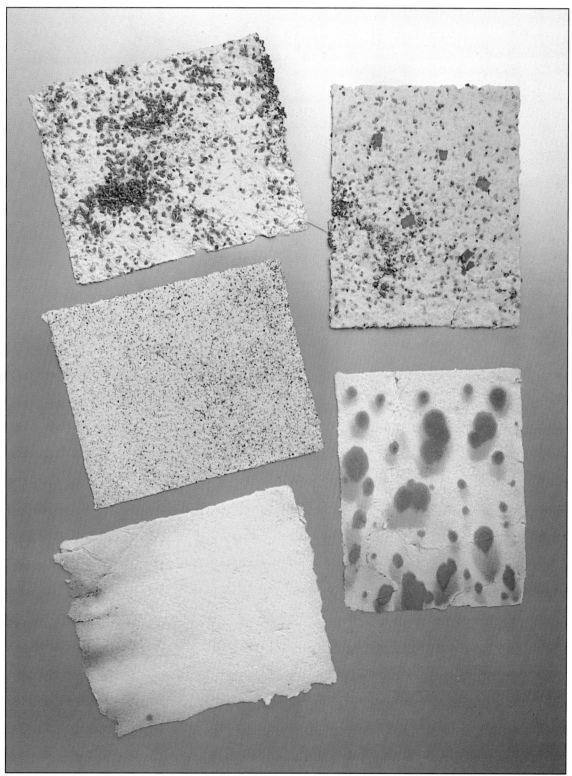

■ DECORATIVE SPONGING

Sponging has been used as a form of decoration for many years, especially on pottery. The process gives a pleasing mottled effect to plain surfaces, and can be very bold and dramatic; or, if you prefer, a more subtle background pattern can also be obtained.

YOU WILL NEED
Selection of poster or gouache paints
Piece of natural sponge
Paper
Newspaper

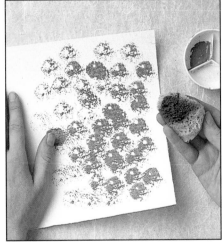

1 Mix a little paint in a saucer or on a small palette. The paint should be fairly sticky. Dip the sponge into the paint and dab it lightly over the surface of the paper, making a random pattern. If you want to be certain of the thickness of the pattern, test the density of the paint first by dabbing the sponge on newspaper.

2 To create patterns with two or more colours, wash the sponge thoroughly and squeeze it almost dry. When the first layer of sponging has dried, add more colours one by one, making sure each has time to dry before the next coat.

RIBBON ROSETTES

Make gifts look extra special with ribbon rosettes that match your wrapping paper. There are many ways of making ribbons into rosettes, pom-poms or just simple bows. Choose from all the types of plain and fancy ribbons available, or make your own by cutting strips from the wrapping paper.

YOU WILL NEED
Ribbon
Double-sided tape

1 Cut eight lengths of ribbon, four 30 cm (12 in) long and the other four measuring 24 cm (9 in). Make each one into a loop by using double-sided tape.

2 Assemble the rosette by crossing two of the longer loops and taping them in the middle. Then make another cross and join to the first cross, making the bottom layer.

3 Repeat with the shorter loops and join these to the base.

4 Finish off by putting a small loop into the centre and fixing it onto your wrapped gift.

5 To make a different ribbon trim, grade the loops to start with a 30 cm (12 in) loop and make each layer smaller by 5 cm (2 in). Holding the loops in the middle, glue them one on top of the other, starting with the largest at the bottom and getting smaller to form a fan shape.

TO MY VALENTINE

This centre opening style of card can be used for any type of message. It could be to wish a Happy Christmas or just an abstract design to say Hello! Some variations are shown below.

YOU WILL NEED
Thin card in two colours
Tissue paper
Glue

1 Take a piece of card 34 × 14 cm (13½ × 5½ in). Instead of folding the card in the usual way, mark the centre of the card and fold each side to the centre point so that they meet. In another colour of card draw and cut out a heart shape. Cut the heart in half.

2 Cut out long strips of tissue paper and fold in half lengthways. Spread glue around the outer edge on the back of the heart shape and then make a frill with the tissue by gathering it up and sticking down. Finally glue both halves of the heart onto the two opening flaps of the card.

CUT-AND-THREAD PAPER

Make plain writing paper extra special with simple strips of crêpe paper threaded through in unusual patterns. Practise first on spare paper to get the right effect.

YOU WILL NEED
Sheet of writing paper
Craft knife
Crêpe paper

1 Take a sheet of writing paper and mark two sets of two vertical lines at the top, in the centre. The lines should be approximately 2 cm (¾ in) long and 2½ cm (1 in) apart. Cut through the lines using a craft knife.

2 Cut a piece of crêpe paper in a toning colour to your writing paper. Thread it under the 'bridges' taking care not to break them.

3 Once the crêpe paper is centred arrange the bow by fanning out the sides.

4 Repeat the bow design on the extended back flap of an envelope to complete the writing set.

5 Another effect can be achieved by marking and cutting out a series of vertical lines across the top of the page. Cut a piece of crêpe paper the same width as the slots, and a thinner strip in a stronger colour.

6 Fold the paper in half to thread the strips through easily, and then open up.

7 Instead of using vertical lines this version uses two staggered lines of horizontal slits. Once again thread the strip of crêpe paper through and see the diagonal pattern it makes.

BLOCK PRINTING

Quite sophisticated printing blocks can be cut from potatoes, and some lovely effects are possible. To make a more permanent block, use pieces of eraser. These can be used with paint or an ink pad.

YOU WILL NEED
Potatoes
Craft knife
Erasers
Poster or gouache paints
Ink pad
Paper
Nail brush
Stiff cardboard

1 To make a potato block, first cut the potato in half, making sure that the cut surface is straight and flat so that the design will print evenly onto the paper. The design can be cut directly into the potato, or else it can be drawn first with a pencil and then carefully pared away using a craft knife. Use the same process to make blocks from erasers.

2 Mix the paint with a little water and dab it onto the surface of the block with a paint brush.

Firmly press the block onto a piece of paper and lift it up again, taking care to use a direct upwards movement to avoid smudging the printed image.

3 Rubber blocks can be used with ink pads as well as with paint.

4 Block printing can be combined with speckling in contrasting colours to create a very lively effect. Here, purple paper with a black block design is speckled using a nail brush dipped in yellow paint. Hold the brush over the paper and draw a piece of stiff cardboard over the bristles, making sure the cardboard is pulled towards the body (to avoid splashing yourself with paint!).

5 Cut a set of symbols into some erasers and use them on letter-heads and envelopes for a personalized look to your stationery.

DECORATIVE
WALLET

Make this tidy wallet out of a favourite colour paper or piece of wrapping paper. You could even design the pattern yourself. Use the wallet to store banknotes, photographs or special letters.

YOU WILL NEED
Stiff paper or wrapping paper
Craft knife
Glue

1 Scale up the template to the size required and transfer the pattern onto the paper. Cut around the edges using a craft knife. Fold the sides inwards and glue one long edge to the other.

2 Glue the bottom flap to seal the end of the wallet, and it is ready for use.

■ 21ST BIRTHDAY POP-UP

This unusual card is perfect for celebrating a special birthday. Once you have mastered the simple pop-up technique you could use different numbers for a variety of birthday years.

YOU WILL NEED
Craft knife
Stiff white and coloured paper
Paints
Glue

2 Next, fold a piece of stiff paper into two to form a card shape. Glue one tab to one half of the backing card, so that the bottom of the crease down the middle of '21' exactly touches the crease on the card.

1 Scale up the '21' shape to the size required and transfer to a piece of white paper. Cut it out using a craft knife and paint the numbers. When the paint is dry, fold the '21' in half and glue the underside of each tab.

3 To finish off, apply glue to the second tab and fold the empty half of the backing card over the top of the second tab. When unfolded, the card will stick to this second tab, pulling up the '21'.

COLLAGE TAGS

When you want to keep things simple and have perhaps used a plain paper to wrap your present, a collaged gift tag can be the perfect finishing touch. They can be as easy or as complicated as you want to make them.

YOU WILL NEED
Orange card
Green paper
Glue
Coloured thread

1 For the Grecian-style tag cut out a Grecian urn and decorative dots in green paper.

2 Glue them onto a folded piece of orange card.

3 Punch a hole and thread through a length of coloured thread.

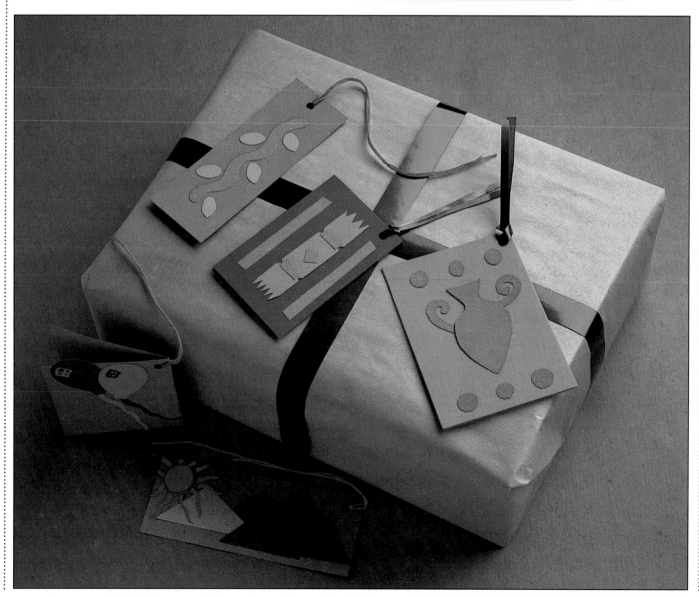

■ WRAPPING A SPHERE

A sphere-shaped present is always a difficult shape to wrap up and it can be approached in two ways. The gift can either be placed in the centre of a piece of paper which can then be gathered up into a bunch above the present and tied with ribbon, or the paper can be pleated. Alternatively, pleat the paper as here.

YOU WILL NEED
Wrapping paper
Sticky tape
Double-sided tape

1 Place the present
■ in the centre of a square piece of paper. Make the square into a circle by rounding off the corners.

2 Start by bringing
■ one section of the paper up to the top. Now work around the circle by pleating the paper so that it

hugs the shape of the sphere. Use tape to secure the pleats as you go round.

3 Continue to pleat
■ neatly until you have gone all the way around. To finish off the top, make a pleated fan.

Take a long strip of paper and fold in half with the right side outside. Pleat the paper along its length.

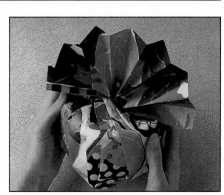

4 Then, pinch the
■ pleats together at the bottom and fan out the sides. Attach it to the present by fixing with double-sided tape.

PLACES ON A THEME

Simple ideas are often the most striking, and so here are some suggestions for place cards made using a collage technique, creating a theme for your table setting.

YOU WILL NEED
Two pieces of contrasting coloured card or paper
Glue
Gold metallic pen
Metallic crêpe paper

1 Draw and cut out a snail shape from coloured paper. Glue it onto the front of a contrasting place card. Use any animal image: you could even give each person an individual animal!

2 For a Mexican theme for your table setting, cut out a cactus shape in green paper or card and stick it onto a yellow place card. Draw on small dots with a gold pen to indicate the prickles.

3 To introduce a touch of frivolity to your table, make up this jolly bow-tie card. Take a rectangle of metallic crêpe paper and fold the ends to the middle. Glue ends in place. Take a smaller strip of crêpe paper and wrap around the centre of the bow to pull into shape. Glue ends in place.

4 Finally glue the bow-tie to the top of the place card.

■ DECORATIVE DOILY

A circle of lightweight coloured card in a contrasting colour forms a base for this tissue paper doily and sets it off to best effect.

YOU WILL NEED
Lightweight card
Tissue paper
Glue

1 To get a good-sized doily, draw around a dinner plate and cut out two circles, one in card and the other in tissue paper.

2 Fold the tissue paper in half three times to form an eighth and cut a scalloped pattern around the curved edge.

3 Fold it in half again and lightly draw a small geometric design along the edge and then cut these shapes out.

4 Unfold back to an eighth of the circle and fold the two edges of the segment to the centre. Draw and cut out your design as before on both edges. Unfold the doily and place on the card for a decorative effect.

CONE HATS

With a simple change of decoration this basic cone hat can make a clown's hat or an elegant medieval headdress fit for a lady.

YOU WILL NEED
Card
Crêpe paper
Glue
Sticky tape

1 For the basic cone you will need to cut out a 60 cm (23 in) diameter semi-circle in card. You can make this measurement larger or smaller depending on the finished size you require. Roll the semi-circle into a cone and fasten with tape or glue.

2 To make the medieval cone cut streamers of crêpe paper in three different colours and push them through the end of the hat. Secure with sticky tape on the inside.

3 Now plait wider strips of the three colours of crêpe paper. Stick the plait onto the base of the cone.

4 To make the clown's hat make up pom-poms by cutting out three 20 cm (8 in) diameter circles of crêpe paper. Pinch each circle in the centre and twist. Now scrunch up the excess paper and mould it into a ball shape.

5 Push the first pom-pom through the top of the cone, then carefully make two slots one above the other down the front of the cone. Push the centre of the pom-poms through the slots and tape them on the inside to secure.

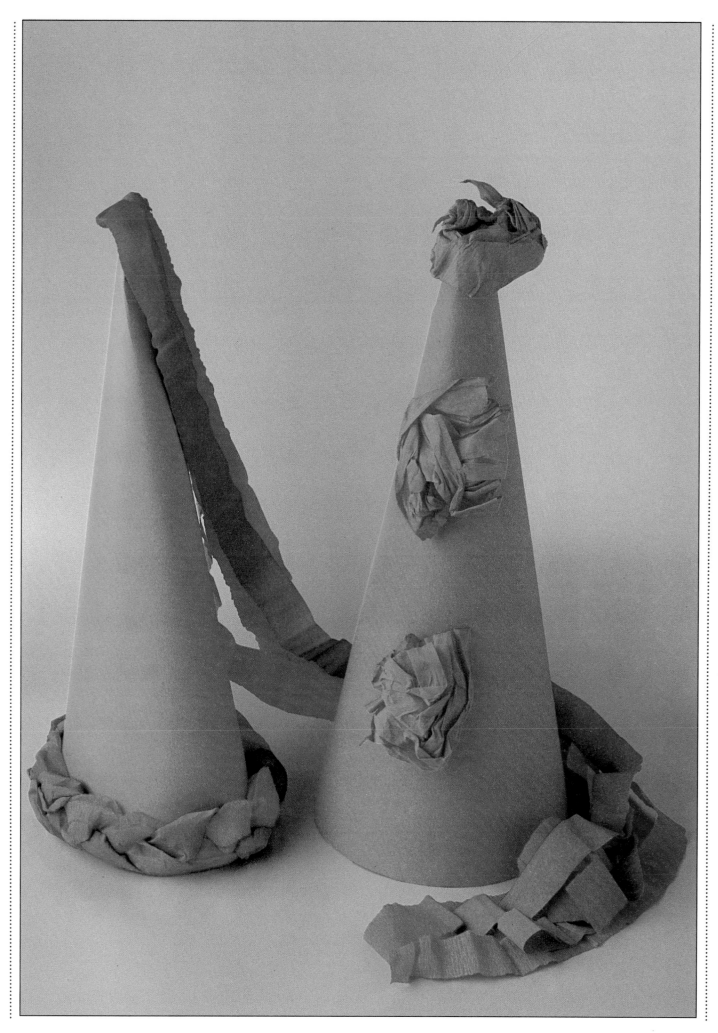

CHRISTMAS GIFT TAGS

If you want to get away from the traditionally shaped gift tag, here is an idea for making them with a stand-out effect.

YOU WILL NEED
Red and green card
Glue
Red paper

1 Take a long strip of red card and fold it so that one end is slightly longer. Draw and cut out a Christmas tree shape on a separate piece of green card.

2 Stick the tree onto the front flap and now cut away the part above the top branches so that it has a shaped top.

3 Then, glue on circles of red paper to decorate the tree.

4 Experiment by making up abstract designs in card, sticking these onto the front and then cutting around the shapes you have created.

SECRET MESSAGES

Give a sense of mystery to your gifts by adding a tag tied with a ribbon bow to conceal your message. A perfect idea for sending notes to loved ones.

YOU WILL NEED
Coloured card
Contrasting coloured paper
Gold metallic pen
Glue
Ribbon

2 On a separate piece of black paper draw a design with a gold pen and stick this onto the card.

1 Take a rectangle of card and fold in half. Open out the card and make a small narrow slit for the ribbon on the centre of both leading edges, back and front.

3 Write your message inside and then thread a length of gold ribbon through the slits and tie a bow to keep the wording a secret.

COMBING AND FEATHERING

Paint can be mixed with cellulose wallpaper paste to make a coloured 'gel' which can be used to create a variety of effects.

YOU WILL NEED
Poster or gouache paints
Large bowl
Cellulose wallpaper paste mixed according to manufacturer's instructions
Paper
Small piece of cardboard
Craft knife
Serrated pottery tools or forks

1 Feathering
■ Add a quantity of paint to the bowl of paste and mix it thoroughly until the desired colour is obtained. Test the depth of colour on a scrap of paper before you use it. Next, take two pieces of paper of the same size (trim if necessary) and, with a paint brush, coat them with a layer of coloured paste.

2 Put one piece of
■ paper on top of the other so that the pasted sides touch. Then gently pull the sheets apart, starting at one corner. This process results in a delicate feathered pattern.

3 Combing
■ To make your own combing implement take a scrap of cardboard and cut 'teeth' into one end using a craft knife. Alternatively, ready-made implements such as pottery tools and forks can be used to achieve the combing effects. First, coat a piece of coloured paper with a layer of the paste. Then draw the combing tool through the paste, leaving behind a trail. This method produces many intricate effects when a variety of tools with different size 'teeth' are used on the same sheet of paper.

■ LIDDED BOX

This box can be used to keep things safe – or to conceal a surprise. Make several in a variety of colours to form a set or give one to each of your friends.

YOU WILL NEED
Thin coloured card
Craft knife
Glue

1 The box and its lid are made in the same way. Scale up the template to the size required and transfer the pattern to thin coloured card. Carefully cut out the pieces using a craft knife. Fold in the side tabs to form the upright sides.

2 Next, assemble the box by applying glue to the central tabs and folding them over the sides, fixing down firmly. Repeat this process to make the lid, and slide it over the base to complete the box.

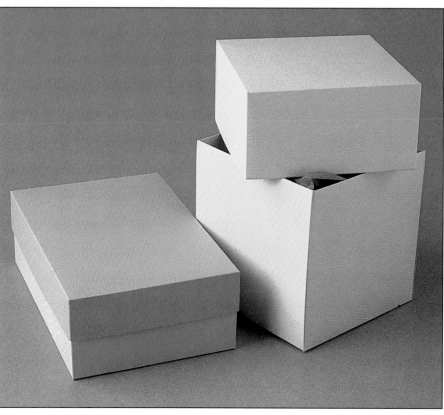

CANDY CONES

Pretty and simple ideas for arranging sweets at a wedding or party. For another alternative wrap a red ribbon upwards around a cone made from elegant wrapping paper and use matching red tissue paper inside.

YOU WILL NEED
Square of wrapping paper
Glue
Rosette
Tissue paper
Sugared almonds

1 All you need is a 20 cm (8 in) square of coloured paper in patterned or plain design. Roll the paper into a cone, starting with a corner and shaping it into a rounded form.

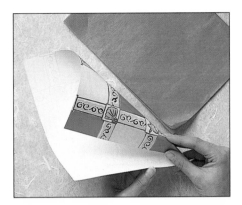

2 Glue the cone together along the edge and stick a rosette on the overlapping point. Flatten the cone at the closed end.

3 Scrunch up some matching tissue paper and push this into the open end. Fill with sugared almonds or candies.

You can vary the design of the cones, depending on the occasion, using different paper and ribbons.

YOU WILL NEED
Black and gold paper
Glue
Ribbon or bow
Tissue paper
Chocolate coins

1 For a variation, cut one square in black paper and another in gold paper. Zigzag the edges along two adjacent sides of the black square, first drawing a line about 1½ cm (¾ in) from the edge as a guideline.

2 Then glue the black paper onto the gold and roll up into a cone form, gluing along the overlapping edges.

3 Slightly flatten the end of the cone and stick on a bow or pieces of ribbon.

4 Take some tissue paper and scrunch it up and insert it into the cone. Fill with chocolate coins.

ACROSS
THE
BORDER

By making the back half of this card slightly wider than the front it enables you to decorate the created border in many ways.

YOU WILL NEED
Assorted coloured paper or card
Silver metallic pen
Glue
Felt-tip pens
Tissue paper

5 This version is slightly more complicated. Take a piece of bright card and fold into the basic shape, then glue a panel of contrasting wrapping paper onto the front. When it is fixed, trim at the sides and then draw an arch and bauble design onto the leading edge. Cut out the arch and bauble shape.

1 To make the basic card fold a rectangle in two so that the top side is slightly shorter than the back.

2 Now shape the front fold by cutting a zigzag border.

3 Stick a contrasting coloured card behind to make the serrated edge stand out.

4 Alternatively, cut out a wavy edge on the front side and then decorate it with a silver line following the curved line. To finish the decoration draw a row of whirls.

6 On the inside of the card glue down a panel of contrasting tissue paper.

7 Cut further small circles in the tissue paper and glue them along the border.

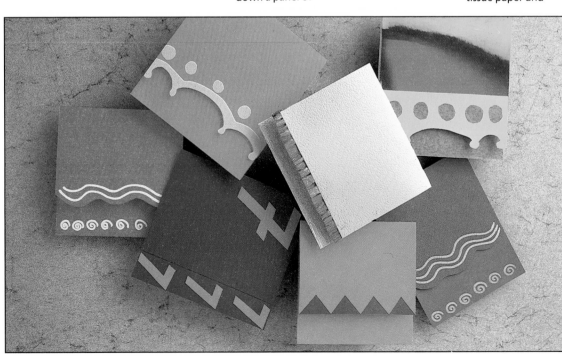

■ S P O T - O N   N A P K I N S

This is a quick and bright way to decorate your paper napkins for children's parties or a special theme dinner. The basic idea is to split the layers of two different coloured napkins, then join them together and cut out shapes in one colour in order to reveal the other.

YOU WILL NEED
Two packets of contrasting coloured paper napkins
Glue

1 Take two paper napkins of different colours. Here a light and a dark colour are used. They should be the same size and preferably the same make so that they fit together exactly. Most napkins are three-ply (three layers). Start by splitting them so that you are working with two layers of each colour. The reason for this is so that the finished napkin is not too thick.

2 Fold the lighter coloured napkin diagonally and cut into two.

3 Carefully glue one half onto the darker napkin. Cut out light-coloured spots from the other half and glue them onto the dark triangle.

4 Now cut out spots from another dark napkin and glue these to the lighter triangle.

GIFT BAG

This gift bag is simple to make and adds a touch of elegance to any present. It can be used instead of separate wrapping paper and is sturdy enough to hold a variety of gifts.

YOU WILL NEED
Decorated paper
Craft knife
Glue
Hole punch
Ribbon

1 Scale up the
■ template to the
size required and
transfer the pattern
onto the decorated
paper. Cut out
carefully using a
craft knife. Score
lightly along the
back of the creases
so that they will fold
more easily. Fold
down and glue the
flaps along the *top*
edge of the bag.

2 Next, glue the
■ long, side tab to
form the bag shape.

3 Then glue the
■ base of the bag,
folding in the short
end tabs first.

4 Form the pleats down the sides of the bag by pressing the long edges together gently so that the paper is pushed inwards.

5 Using the hole punch, make two holes on each of the top sides near the upper edge. Cut two short lengths of ribbon and thread each end through the holes to make two looped handles. Knot the ends at the back of the holes to secure.

STENCIL STYLE

Use ready-made or cut your own stencils to make this stylish writing paper. Dab on stencil paints or colour with soft crayons for speedy results.

YOU WILL NEED
Stencilling card
Craft knife
Paint
Stencil brush
Writing paper
Crayon

1 Using the template transfer the motif onto stencilling card in the size you require and cut out using a craft knife.

2 Prepare the paint on a saucer and collect the colour onto a stencil brush. Then, holding the stencilling card firmly with one hand, use the other to dab the brush onto the writing paper using a circular movement.

3 Instead of using paint, a coloured crayon could be used. Once again hold the stencilling card firmly in one hand and lightly fill in the pattern, remembering to work the crayon strokes in the same direction each time.

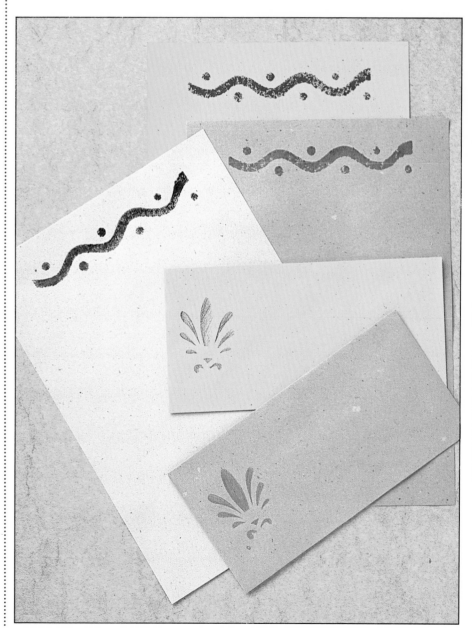

PLACES PLEASE!

Here is a selection of attractive name cards for the table, using a technique of slotting decorative paper shapes through the card to create an interesting three-dimensional effect. Experiment with your own ideas!

YOU WILL NEED
Black, orange and white card
Craft knife
Red, orange and green paper
Sticky tape
Wrapping paper
Glue
Crêpe paper
Gold metallic pen

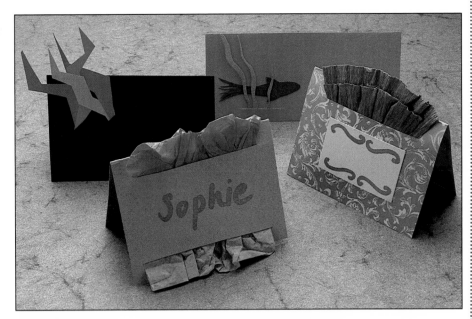

1 First, fold a piece of black card, 13 × 10 cm (5 × 4 in) in half lengthways. Open out again and place flat. On the bottom half of the card, cut two short lines just above each other in the top left hand corner area, using a craft knife. Then, cut out flame shapes in red and orange paper.

2 Push the flame shapes through the slots, from the back to the front of the card, and arrange so that they extend at varying angles and lengths.

3 Turn the card over, and secure the ends on the back with sticky tape.

4 For this fishy collage card, make an orange card and glue on a green fish. Cut a slot at the bottom of the card. Cut wavy strips of green paper for weeds, and push them up through the slot and arrange. Secure on the back as before.

5 As a decorative alternative, you could cover the card with patterned wrapping paper. Fold the card in half, then cut a long slot in the top edge of the front side. Cut two lengths of crêpe paper twice as long as the slot and fold up to make a frill, a little longer than the slot. Push the frills through the slot. Secure at the back with tape as before. To complete, stick a small piece of white card in the centre, and decorate with a gold pen.

NOTELET HOLDER

Take an ordinary writing pad and envelopes and dress them up in a special notelet holder. All kinds of versions are possible, made from decorative papers and cards.

YOU WILL NEED
Writing paper and envelopes
Card
Glue
Brown paper or wrapping paper
Gold metallic pen
String
2 paper fasteners

1 To make the notelet holder use one of the envelopes to determine the size, and cut a piece of card, measuring the length of the envelope and adding 8 cm (3 in), by three times the height of the envelope plus 8 cm (3 in).

2 Cut out the card with or without the pointed flap according to the finished style that you require.

3 Apply glue to the unmarked side of the cut out card, and then cover in brown paper, trimming the edges where necessary. In this example the paper covering is decorated by hand, but you could use a favourite wrapping paper or a piece of wallpaper.

4 Taking a gold pen draw a design onto the brown paper.

5 On the inside, score along the marked lines and cut the tab lines.

7 Decorate the brown paper with the gold pen as before. Fold the paper in half and pop the six notelets and envelopes into the notelet holder.

6 To make the notelets take six sheets of paper from the writing pad and glue a piece of brown paper or wrapping paper onto each sheet of writing paper. Trim to size.

8 Now fold and glue the notelet holder together. To make the closure push the fasteners through the paper at the point of envelope flap and in the front of the box to one side of the flap. Secure the case with a loop of string round the fasteners.

CONCENTRIC TWIST

Hang this impressive paper sculpture in a window; if it is made from metallic-coated card it will catch the light as it moves gently in the air currents.

YOU WILL NEED
Thin coloured card
Craft knife

1 Scale up the template to the required size and transfer to coloured card. Cut the slits using a craft knife. Gently twist the central circle away from its frame.

2 Starting at the rim, form the first twist again by gently turning the central section at an angle of 90 degrees to the outer ring.

3 Continue to form the twists by turning each ring at the same angle, moving progressively towards the centre, until the twist-out is complete.

3-D CHRISTMAS TREE

Make a paper Christmas tree stand out by adding extra layers. Smother it with self-adhesive stars for a quick and easy decorative touch.

YOU WILL NEED
Coloured card in three colours
Glue
Self-adhesive stars
Ribbon

1 Cut out three Christmas tree shapes, in three different colours, so that they are gradually smaller in size.

2 Now cut twelve small squares of card and glue six of them together one on top of the other to make a block. Glue the other six in the same way. Glue one card block onto the top of the largest tree and the second one onto the middle-sized tree.

3 Glue the tip of the middle-sized tree onto the largest tree and the smallest tree onto the top of the middle-sized tree.

4 Now decorate all three trees with sticky stars. Attach a ribbon at the back so that it can be hung up to be displayed.

ABSTRACT POP-UP

This stunning pop-up sculpture is always impressive. Once you have mastered the basic technique you can start to experiment with your own designs.

YOU WILL NEED
Sheet of stiff paper
Metal rule
Craft knife
Sharp blade

1 Scale up the template to the size required and transfer onto the paper. Place a metal rule or other strong, straight edge along each strip and cut through each line with a craft knife.

2 Next, score along all the short creases with a scissor blade or similar implement, taking care not to cut right through the paper.

3 Take the piece of paper in both hands and very carefully begin to bend the pop-up in half. The strips of paper should begin to bend outwards but remain parallel to each other.

4 Close the two sides of the sheet of paper, ensuring that all the strands are lying side by side, folded evenly.

5 Lay the paper flat and, using gentle pressure, push down on all the creases to strengthen them. Open out the card and watch the design appear.

PRACTICAL ENVELOPE

Home-made envelopes can be cheaper and a lot more fun than shop-bought ones. Make a set from a variety of different papers, both plain and patterned. In order to write the address on a patterned paper simply add a little white label.

YOU WILL NEED
Stiff paper
Glue

1 Scale up the template to the size required and transfer to the stiff paper. Using a scissor blade, gently score along the back of the creases that are to be folded. Next, fold in the side flaps.

2 Glue the bottom flap to the side flaps to form the envelope. Pop in your letter or card, seal with a dab of glue and send it off!

RING THE CHANGES

Using small pieces of coloured card you can create several different eyecatching napkin rings. Add contrasting coloured motifs, or simply cut and slot them into interesting shapes.

YOU WILL NEED
Coloured card
Contrasting coloured paper
Glue

1 Take a plain band of card measuring 15 × 5 cm (6 × 2 in). For the classical column design cut out the 'capital' and 'flutes' from contrasting colour paper and stick them onto the plain strip.

2 When the strip has been decorated, dab some glue onto one end and bring the other end around to join. Hold the ends in place until the glue has dried.

3 For the blue napkin ring, shape the ends by drawing and cutting out a design, so that when the ends are brought together the band looks more interesting.

4 To finish off add a contrasting colour circle with a blue dot in the centre.

5 For the asymmetrical rings, take a strip the same size as before and cut a 4 cm (1¼ in) slot, 1 cm (⅜ in) in from the end and parallel to it. Repeat the same on the other end but making sure that the slot is cut from the opposite edge.

6 Now cut the ends and interlink the slots so that they hold together. Decorate the ends by fringing or cutting triangles in them. By varying the size of the darts you can experiment with different effects.

▪ BOW-TIE GIFTWRAP

Here is an interesting way to present your gifts by making your own three-dimensional bow-tie wrapping paper.

YOU WILL NEED
Crêpe paper in two or three contrasting colours
Double-sided tape or glue

1 First wrap your gift in a plain crêpe paper. To make the bows, cut out 5 cm (2 in) wide strips of contrasting crêpe paper and then cut them into 6 cm (2½ in) lengths.

2 Gather each piece in the middle and then twist to make the bow shape.

3 Now attach the bows to the wrapped gift either with double-sided tape or some glue.

4 To make your present really stand out, make up the bows in two different colours twisted together.

CUT-OUT STATIONERY

A fleur-de-lys motif is used for this writing paper cut-out, but you could choose a simple heart shape or your initial as decoration.

YOU WILL NEED
Plain writing paper
Craft knife
Contrasting coloured paper
Glue

1 Scale the motif from the template up or down to the required size or design your own and transfer it onto the centre of the top of the writing paper.

2 Carefully cut out the background area with a craft knife. Using a pair of scissors cut out a small rectangle of a different coloured card just larger than the motif.

3 Turn the writing paper over, glue around the opening and then stick down the contrasting coloured card. Turn the paper back again and see how the motif stands out.

■ T E A R I N G   H U R R Y

Using pieces of torn paper to create an abstract design, these cards are unusual and unique! Experiment with colours and cards for the best effect.

YOU WILL NEED
Envelope
Card
Ruler
Craft knife
Paper scraps
Glue

1 Using the size of an envelope as a guide, cut out a piece of complementary card three times as wide. Divide and mark the card into three equal parts. In the central panel cut out an opening with a ruler and a craft knife to create the frame.

2 Tear up pieces of paper into similarly-sized, irregular shapes and start to arrange them on the left hand panel.

3 Once you are happy with the arrangement of the collage pieces they can be glued into position. Complete the card by gluing around the frame in the centre panel and sticking it down over the artwork. Fold the blank sheet round to form the card shape and add your message.

DESK TIDY

Simple boxes can be used for many purposes; this one is ideal for keeping all those essential bits and pieces in one place on a desk.

YOU WILL NEED
Thin card
Craft knife
Glue

1 Scale up the pattern to the size required. Transfer onto a piece of thin card and cut it out using a craft knife. First of all fold in the side tabs.

2 Next, 'lock' the box by applying glue to the central tab and folding it over the side tabs, sticking it down firmly. Fill the box with pencils, pens and ink or other useful items.

ANTIQUE MARBLING

There are several methods of marbling paper to achieve the beautiful effects seen on old bookbinding and traditional Italian stationery. The process involves suspending pigment on top of water, arranging the colour into patterns, and transferring these to paper.

YOU WILL NEED
Metal roasting pan or deep tray
Paper
Oil paints in various colours
White spirit
Paint brush or metal skewer

1 Half fill a clean metal roasting pan or a deep tray with cold water. Cut a piece of paper to fit the size of the tray. Thin a little oil paint with white spirit, and dot the diluted paint onto the surface of the water with a brush.

2 The paint will disperse, creating patterns on the surface of the water. Hold the paper by the top right- and bottom left-hand corners and lower it across the surface of the water in a rolling movement.

3 Carefully lift the paper from the tray. The paint will adhere to the paper, giving a marbled effect. Lay the sheets out to dry at room temperature.

4 To create multi-coloured patterns add two or more colours of oil paint to the surface of the water. Use the end of a paint brush or a metal skewer to move the colours around before laying the paper down on the water. Before marbling subsequent pieces of paper, skim the surface of the water with scrap paper to pick up excess paint and keep the water clean.

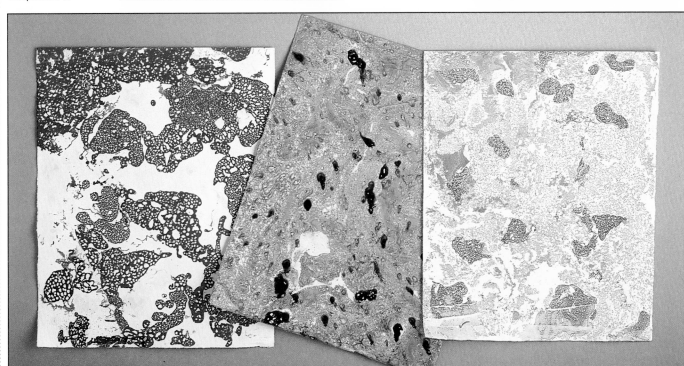

ONE-PIECE GIFT BOXES

This box is constructed from a single piece of card and can be closed tightly, making it an ideal container, either vertical or horizontal, for sweets or small biscuits.

YOU WILL NEED
Thin card
Craft knife
Glue

Vertical version

Horizontal version

1 Scale up the template to the size required, and transfer it to the card. Cut it out using a craft knife. Score along the back folds of the tabs. Fold up the sides of the box and glue the end tab to make a tube shape.

2 Interlock the tabs at the base of the box and the base should lock securely without glue.

VALENTINE'S HEART

This pop-up surprise will add a touch of fun to Valentine's Day. The same technique can be used to make cards for other occasions, such as a tree for Christmas time, or a house for a friend's moving day.

YOU WILL NEED
Stiff paper in two different colours
Glue

3ins
8cms

Support

2¼ins
7cms

1 Scale up the support from the template to the required size and cut out of a piece of stiff paper. Then fold a matching piece of paper into two halves to form a card. Fold the support to the correct shape, creasing the tabs upwards.

2 Next, glue the support to the backing card near the top, ensuring that the crease on the support exactly touches the crease on the card. Note that the support is symmetrically placed over the crease.

3 Cut out a heart shape in red paper and glue it to the tabs at the top of the support. Decorate the inside border of the card to match. When the card is opened the heart will spring out and surprise the recipient!

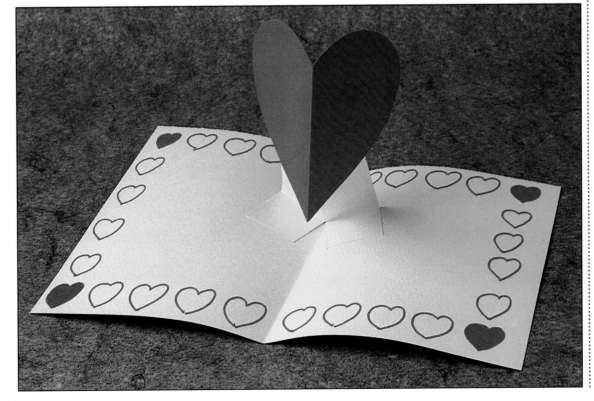

EGYPTIAN EVENING

Ancient Egypt is the inspiration for this exotic place setting of place mat, napkin holder and name card embellished in bronze and gold.

YOU WILL NEED
Thin card
Bronze, black and blue paper
Glue
Gold metallic pen
Black felt-tip pen (optional)
Sticky tape

1 Place mat
■ In order to make up this place mat, cut out a piece of card in the shape of a Pharoah's head which should measure 30 cm (12 in) across the bottom and have a height of 27 cm (11 in). Cover the card in bronze coloured paper and, in the centre area, very lightly mark out the shape of the face in pencil. Cut the beard out of black paper, glue in place, and then make a criss-cross design on it with a gold pen. Scale up to the size required the features of the face from the template and cut out of black paper and glue into position or use a black felt-tip pen to draw them in.

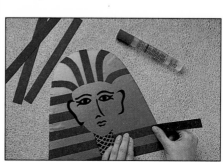

2
Cut strips of blue paper 2 cm (¾ in) wide for the headdress decoration and start to glue them in parallel lines onto the bronze card. The strips at the top of the head are slightly curved. Add blue dots for the earrings.

3 Napkin holder
■ To make the Egyptian napkin holder, first cut out an 18 cm (7 in) square of card. Cover one side in bronze paper and the other side in black paper. Fold up one side not quite half-way, with the bronze side inside, and add blue strips, fanning them out as shown. Trim the strips level with the edge of card. Cut out an Egyptian eye motif in bronze paper and fix it onto the front.

4 Name place card
■ Cut out two triangles in card. Cover one side in black paper. Join them at the top by cutting off the top corner and taping them together at the back. Cut out a bronze motif, glue on the front then use a gold pen to write on the names required.

DECORATIVE PAPERCRAFTS

BROWN PAPER STATIONERY

Sometimes you need very little to make a good impression. For this project recycled brown paper is used to decorate the sheets of writing paper.

YOU WILL NEED
Brown paper
Plain writing paper
Glue
Gold metallic pen
Black felt-tip pen

1 For the first idea, tear a thin strip of the brown paper and glue it down, either on the right-hand side of the page or across the top as illustrated.

2 Then take a gold pen and draw a design along the strip. Remember that you can invent your own designs.

3 As an alternative suggestion, stick down pieces of brown paper to make two corner strips. Take the gold pen, draw in a design and then give it a three-dimensional effect by outlining it in a black felt-tip pen.

4 Another variation on the same theme is to tear a wider strip of brown paper and then tear it into four squares. Glue these down at the top of the paper and then decorate with black spots using a felt-tip pen.

FLOWER POWER

A simple idea for a get well or Mother's Day card. As an alternative, choose yellow backing paper for a birthday design.

YOU WILL NEED
Thin card in three colours
Craft knife
Glue

1 Take a rectangle of card and fold it in half. Draw the 'daisy' pattern onto one half of the card and with the card opened out flat cut out the shapes using a craft knife.

2 Cut a piece of pink card to the same size as the folded card. On the inside of the main card spread glue around the cut-out areas and place over the pink card.

3 Cut out orange circles from the remaining card and glue in place to make the centres of the daisies.

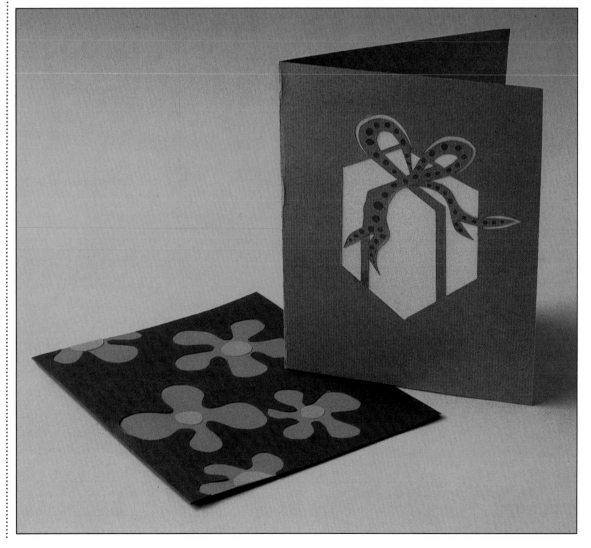

■ F R U I T ' N ' V E G

Here is a fruity number that makes a collection of fun gift tags. These are just a few ideas from the wide variety of interesting shapes that can be found in fruit and vegetables, such as peas and bananas.

YOU WILL NEED
Orange, green and yellow card
Sticky tape
Coloured felt-tip pens

1 For a carrot gift
▬ tag scale up the
template and
transfer to the
orange card. Cut out
the pair of carrots,
making sure that the
top is not cut in
order to leave the
fold intact. Now cut
out some greenery.

2 Open out the
▬ card and cut two
slots with a craft
knife at the top of
the carrots.

3 Next, push the
▬ greenery through
the slots and secure
on the back with
some tape.

4 The last stage is
▬ to draw the
shading marks onto
the carrot with a
brown felt-tip pen.

■ BEAUTIFUL BINDING

If you have an old book or album and want to brighten them up you can learn how to cover your own pages. For this project you will need to determine the size of your book. If you are making a photograph album, for instance, the size will be determined by the album pages.

YOU WILL NEED
Book or photograph album
Thick card
Adhesive cloth tape
Patterned and plain wrapping paper
Glue
Hole punch
Ribbon

1 First cut two pieces of thick card that are about 1 cm (½ in) wider and longer than the pages to be covered. If you are covering a loose-leaf album, measure the side strip of the album sheet which has the holes punched in it, and mark the same amount onto the top of one of the cards, which will eventually be the top cover. Cut a small strip off one side of this.

2 Using the other back card as a measure, place the trimmed top card onto it and put the narrow strip above so that there is a gap between them where the strip has been removed. Tape the pieces together using adhesive cloth tape. Turn the block over and put another piece of the cloth tape onto the other side. This will make the hinge for the top cover.

3 Now glue on a decorative paper to cover the outsides. A toning or contrasting plain colour is used to cover the inside.

4 Next lay an album or page sheet on to the bottom cover and draw where the holes are onto it. Punch them through using a hole punch. Repeat the process with the front cover.

5 Now place the pages onto the back cover so that the holes are aligned and put the front cover on top. To finish off, thread a good quality ribbon through the holes.

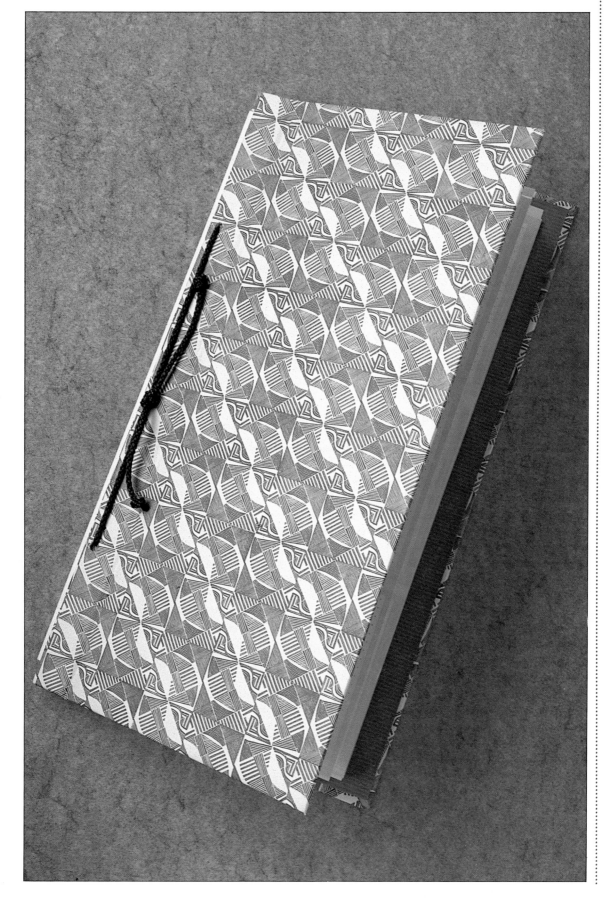

■ MARBLED TAGS

Inevitably, after wrapping presents with marbled or decorated paper, there are small scraps left over that are too large to justify throwing away. Matching gift tags will make good use of these scraps as well as brightening up your present even further. You could even make them into a collection of ten gift tags and present them as a gift for a friend.

YOU WILL NEED
Marbled wrapping paper
Contrasting coloured card
Glue
Ribbon

1 First of all cut out
■ some interesting shapes from the left-over marbled paper.

2 Then choose
■ some contrasting coloured card which will bring out the beautiful colours in the marbelling. Glue the marbled motif onto the card and trim the card to suit the shape of the motif.

3 Make a hole in
■ the tag to thread some ribbon through.

■ STAND-UP PLACE NAMES

Make your place cards really stand out with these novelty motifs that project above the cards. Choose simple, recognizable shapes cut out from contrasting coloured card.

YOU WILL NEED
Green, orange, red and white card
Glue
Gold metallic pen
Craft knife

1 Take a square of green card and fold in half. Cut out an octopus shape from orange card but instead of gluing it directly onto the green card, position it so that the top half is above the fold line. Cut out the facial features from the green card and glue in place.

2 For a festive name place, cut out two holly leaves in green. Fix them onto the top of a red place card so that the holly is sticking upwards. Cut out and glue on red dots to make the berries.

3 To make this rocket name card, fold then unfold the name card and lay flat. Draw on the spaceship shape onto the lower half with gold pen so that the top of the rocket extends over the halfway line. With a craft knife, cut around the top part of the rocket only. Then fold the card in half again and the rocket will stand up.

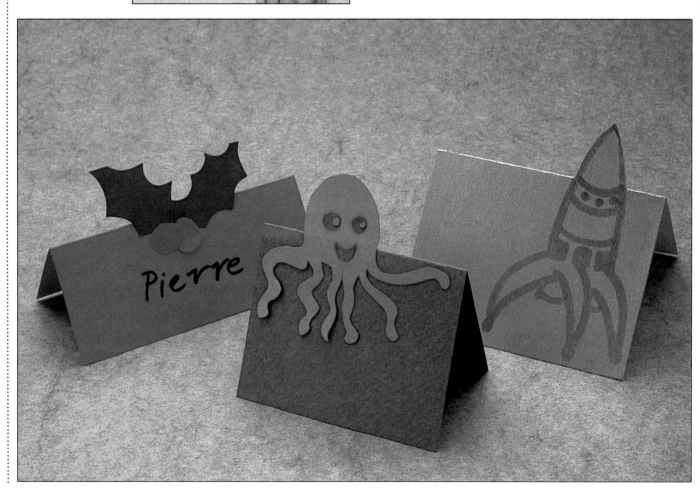

LOCKING BAG

This bag has a flap which 'locks', keeping the contents safe inside. Choose a favourite paper or decorate plain paper with your own design.

YOU WILL NEED
Decorated paper
Craft knife
Glue

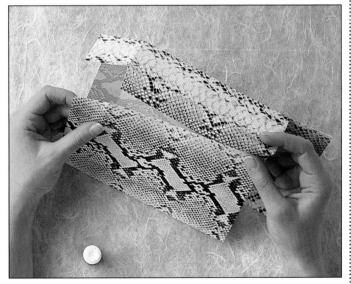

1 Scale up the template to the size required and transfer it to the decorated paper. Cut out the shape using a craft knife. Score along the back edges of the creases to allow them to fold more easily. Fold down and glue all flaps along the *top* edge except for the lid flap.

2 Next, glue the end tab to form the bag shape.

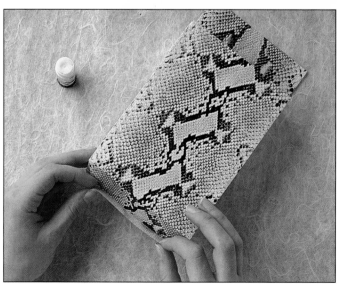

3 Glue the base of
the bag, folding
in the short end tabs
first.

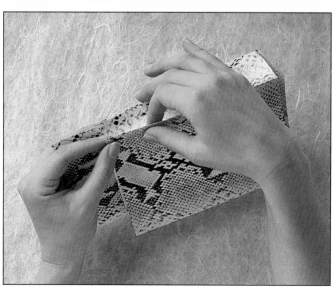

4 Form the pleats
down the short
sides of the bag by
gently pressing the
long edges together
so that the paper
inbetween is pushed
inwards. Close the
top by folding the
excess tab down into
the *front* half of
each pleat.

SCULPTURED TOPS

For this style of card it is best to have a tall image so that the majority of the folded card remains intact and is able to stand up. A palm tree card is described here, but you could use similar techniques to create the architectural variations shown.

YOU WILL NEED
Assorted coloured card
Orange and brown
*   paper*
Glue

1 Take a square of coloured card and fold in half. Draw out the shape of the palm tree leaves on the front and cut out the uppermost ones through both layers.

2 Then cut out coconuts from orange and brown paper and stick them onto the card at the base of the leaves.

3 Draw a tree trunk shape on light green card and cut out. Cut a zigzag edge along one side and glue this onto the card.

ENVELOPE LETTERS

There is no need for an envelope if you make this clever stationery that folds up like a notelet. Seal it with a sequin and pop it in the post.

YOU WILL NEED
Sheet of writing paper
Glue
Sequin
Double-sided tape

1 Fold a sheet of writing paper into three parts so that the top third is slightly smaller than the others.

2 On the top fold draw a line from the centre to each corner to make an envelope flap and then cut off the corner triangles.

3 To decorate the top, glue a sequin at the point. A piece of gold, metallic or shiny card would work as well.

4 Just under the flap attach a small piece of double-sided sticky tape and then draw in address lines on the reverse.

5 There are lots of different ways to decorate the envelope letter. You can glue on strips of contrasting coloured paper so that when the paper is folded up it looks like a present.

Paper Projects

TIGER, TIGER

Dress up as a big cat with this colourful tiger mask that will set the scene for a jungle theme party.

YOU WILL NEED
Orange card
Black felt-tip pen
Black ribbon
Craft knife
Sticky tape
Sewing needle
Elastic

3 For the whiskers cut thin strips of black ribbon about 12 × ½ cm (5 × ¼ in). Using a craft knife make four small slots on either side of the nose.

4 Push the whisker strips through the slots and use tape on the back to secure them.

1 Use the template, scaled up to size required, and cut out the tiger mask in some bright orange card.

2 Now draw on the tiger stripes with a black felt-tip pen.

5 Now sew on some elastic to either side of the mask and adjust to fit.

EASTER EGG BASKET

Make Easter egg-stra special by giving this pretty gift-wrapped basket of eggs. Choose daffodil yellow card and tissue, or bright pink as here.

YOU WILL NEED
Old bowl-shaped container
Coloured card
Glue
Metallic tissue paper
Pink tissue paper
Pink ribbon
Chocolate eggs

1 Cut a strip of card large enough to go around the bowl and just a bit deeper. Then cut a wavy line along the top edge.

2 Glue the strip onto the bowl.

3 Now take a square of metallic tissue paper and place it in the bottom of the bowl.

4 Scrunch up a large sheet of bright pink tissue paper and arrange it in the bottom of the bowl. Place the chocolate eggs inside on the pink tissue paper. Bring the metallic tissue paper around and tie together with some pink ribbon.

CHOCOLATE BOX

This box is quick and easy to assemble. It needs only a spot of glue and a few tucks. Fill it with chocolates or homemade truffles for the perfect gift.

YOU WILL NEED
Thin coloured card
Craft knife
Glue

1 First, scale up the pattern from the template to the size required and transfer to the piece of card. Cut out using a craft knife, scoring along the back of the creases. Glue the end tab to form the basic box shape.

2 Next, interlock the tabs at the base of the box. If the pattern has been carefully cut out, the base will lock strongly without glue. Fill the box with sweets and fold down the lid.

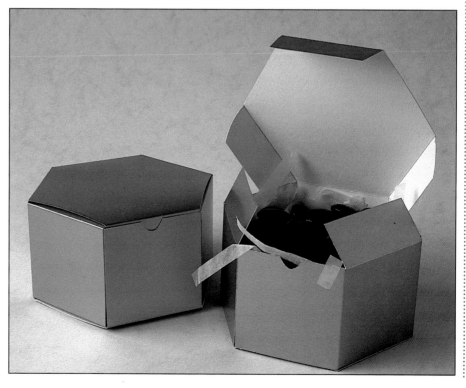

RING AND BANGLE

A very simple way to make attractive jewellery is by twisting paper. Sheets of newspaper are twisted into a tight 'rope' and fitted around the wrist or throat to form bangles and rings, which can be covered with papier-mâché and decorated.

YOU WILL NEED
Newspaper
Masking tape
Diluted PVA glue
Fine sandpaper
White paint
Selection of poster paints
Glass 'gems', sequins, shells etc.
Non-toxic clear gloss varnish

1 Ring
▬ Take quarter of a sheet of newspaper and roll and twist it into a thin rope. Secure the rope along its length with strips of masking tape. Hold the rope around your finger, cut it to size, and tape the ends firmly together.

2 Tear small thin ▬ strips of news-paper, about 1 × 5 cm (½ × 2 in), coat them with diluted PVA glue, and stick them around the ring. Three layers of papier-mâché strips will be sufficient.

3 To add decorative ▬ knobbles to the ring, perhaps to imitate jewels, squash short pieces of newspaper between your fingers to form pellets, and stick in place.

4 Allow the ring to ▬ dry for 24 hours in a warm place. Lightly sand down the ring, and prime it with two coats of white paint.

5 Bangle
▬ To make the bangle, simply roll up a double sheet of newspaper to make a thicker rope, cut it to fit your wrist and then follow the same process you used to make the ring. Decorate the ring and bangle with poster paints. You may like to paint them in one colour, and then augment them with sequins, 'gems' or shells. Leave them to dry overnight, and then seal with two coats of non-toxic clear gloss varnish.

PLAQUE

Your family may have a coat of arms or a heraldic device that could be displayed on a wall plaque – if it hasn't, why not invent one? Add a Latin motto or phrase for authenticity – the wittier the better!

YOU WILL NEED
Thick cardboard
Strong clear glue
Masking tape
Diluted PVA glue
2 picture hangers
Newspaper
Fine sandpaper
White paint
Selection of poster paints
Non-toxic clear gloss varnish
Chain or cord to hang plaque

1 Cut three identical pieces of cardboard to the required dimensions, and stick them together with strong clear glue, securing the edges with masking tape. Paint the plaque with a coat of diluted PVA glue and allow it to dry. Stick two picture hangers to the reverse of the plaque with strong clear glue, and secure the stem of each hanger with a piece of masking tape.

2 Next, let the glue behind the hangers dry for at least an hour, and then cover the plaque with five layers of papier-mâché, using strips of newspaper approximately 2½ cm (1 in) wide, soaked in PVA glue.

3 Lightly sand down the surface of the plaque, and then apply two layers of white paint. Leave time for the paint to dry thoroughly.

4 Finally, draw in your design with pencil, and decorate the plaque with poster paints. Seal the finished plaque with two coats of non-toxic clear gloss varnish. Attach a chain or cord to the hangers on the reverse side to suspend it from the wall.

F R A M E D
P I E C E

If you have a spare frame or a gap on a wall that you have been wondering how to fill, here is a way to make a charming abstract seashore scene. You can vary the images to make a series of pieces for different sized frames.

YOU WILL NEED
Stencilling card
Craft knife
Assortment of coloured papers
Glue

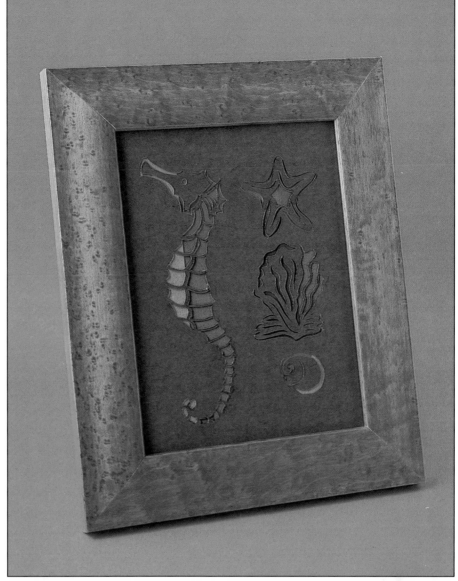

1 Scale up the design on the template to the size that you require for your frame. Draw it out onto a piece of stencilling card and carefully cut out the lines using a craft knife so that the shapes show through. Take care not to cut through any 'bridges' in the card.

2 Next, place the cut-out stencil onto the piece of coloured paper which will form the main background. Then cut out squares or rectangles of different coloured papers until you have enough to fill the spaces in the stencil design.

3 Arrange the coloured papers by placing them between the stencilling card and the background paper and see how they give form to the shapes.

4 When you have decided on the colours for the final picture, glue all the pieces into position. Finally, trim the pieces of coloured paper that extend beyond the stencil and secure the picture into a frame.

PIRATES AHOY!

This hat is simple to make, but looks good and would make a very realistic pirate outfit. For added authenticity cut out an eye patch and tie with elastic.

YOU WILL NEED
Gold card
Stiff black paper
White paint
Double-sided tape
Black elastic

1 Cut out a strip of gold card measuring 6 × 60 cm (2¼ × 23½ in) and join the ends together to make the basic headband.

2 Next cut out two pirate hat shapes in stiff black paper. On the front piece mark out a skull and cross bones (the pirate's hallmark) and paint it in white.

3 Apply two pieces of double-sided tape to the back and front of the headband and stick on the black paper hat shapes.

4 Now stick a small square of double-sided tape at either end of the hat so that the back and front sides join together.

5 For the eye patch, cut out a small triangle in the same black paper just large enough to fit over your eye. Attach elastic to either side so that it can be worn around your head to make the eye patch.

■ CHRISTMAS
TREE GIFT BOX

Here is a way to make a very attractive
Christmas decoration to hang on the
tree. Pop a sweet or small gift inside or
leave it empty simply for decoration.

YOU WILL NEED
White card
Craft knife
Ruler
Glue
Wrapping paper
Ribbon

1 Using the
template, scaled
to the size required,
draw and cut out the
box shape in white
card. You can make
it smaller or larger
by altering the size
of the square as you
like.

2 Score along all
the lines using a
craft knife and ruler,
taking care not to
cut through the card
completely.

3 Shape the box by
folding the sides
up along the scored
lines. Apply glue to
the tabs and hold
the box in position
until it is fixed.

4 Now cover the
box in an
appropriate
wrapping paper.

5 Finish off by tying
a ribbon
decoratively, and
making a loop to
hang the box on the
tree.

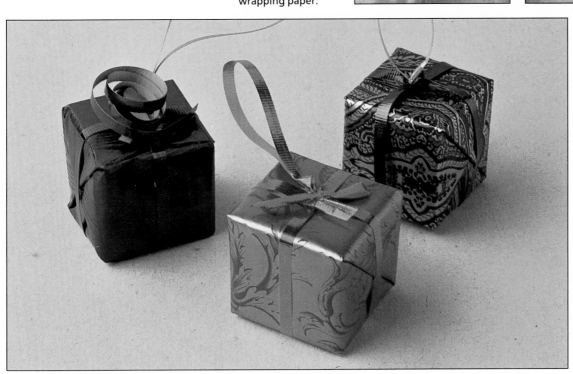

PAPIER-MÂCHÉ PUPPET

Papier-mâché has long been associated with puppet-making, being a cheap, lightweight alternative to wood or clay. The simple construction of this puppet makes it easy to handle, and sumptuous costumes can be made out of exotic fabric scraps.

YOU WILL NEED
Newspaper
Masking tape
Diluted PVA glue
Fine sandpaper
White paint
Selection of poster paints
Black ink (optional)
Non-toxic clear gloss varnish
Piece of doweling rod about 40 cm (16 in) long
Thin string
Strong clear glue
Scraps of fabric, torn or cut into strips

1 Beginning with the puppet's head, crumple a double newspaper page into a ball, then sculpt it with masking tape into the desired shape. Do not forget to give your puppet a neck, as the top of the doweling crossbar will be glued inside.

2 Tear newspaper into strips and soak in diluted PVA glue. Cover the puppet's head with four layers of papier-mâché.

3 Form the puppet's features by squashing glue-soaked strips of newspaper into small pellets of pulp and sticking them in place. Cover over the pulp with two layers of short thin newspaper strips.

4 Allow the head to dry overnight in a warm place. Lightly smooth it with fine sandpaper and then prime it with two coats of white paint. When it is quite dry, draw in the puppet's features, and decorate the head with poster paints, adding detail with black ink if desired. Let the head dry overnight and seal it with two coats of clear gloss varnish.

5 Cut the doweling rod into two pieces 10 cm (4 in) and 30 cm (12 in) long. Place the shorter piece of rod across the longer piece, and tie them together in a cross. Make a hole in the puppet's neck and glue in the rod. Leave in a warm place to dry overnight.

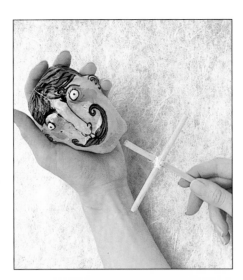

6 Finally, tear or cut strips of fabric about 2½ cm (1 in) wide and long enough to cover the doweling rod. Tie the strips along the length of crossbar that forms the puppet's arms. You might like to tie some fabric around the puppet's neck as well, to disguise the point where it joins the rod.

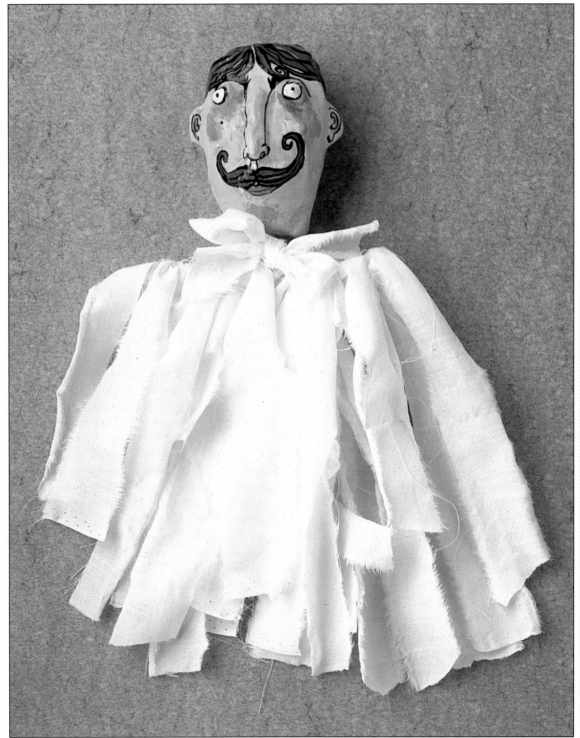

M A S K

This handsome king mask could be used for plays or pantomimes, or for fancy-dress parties. It is made from heavy-weight paper and is strong but still flexible. By using the same basic face shape, and changing the crown to hair or a hat, you could make all sorts of masks, both male and female. Remember to cut the chin round rather than pointed if you do not want the mask to have a beard!

YOU WILL NEED
Thick paper in various colours
Gold paper
Glue
Thin elastic
Darning needle

1 Scale up the basic mask shapes from the template to the size required, and transfer them to appropriately coloured papers. Carefully cut out the shapes.

2 Next, take the face shape and stick the nose, beard and gold crown onto it using a thin coating of glue.

3 Decorate using smaller pieces of coloured paper. Embellish the crown with jewels, and define the beard with strips of lighter coloured paper. Before wearing, carefully push a length of thin elastic through the mask using a darning needle. Knot the ends inside the mask.

■ SPOTTY DOG

This spotty dog is made from tightly rolled and twisted newspaper. It is a very good method for the construction of other animals, giving a firm armature or support for papier-mâché. It might be fun to make a giraffe or an elephant to go into a papier-mâché ark!

YOU WILL NEED
Newspaper
Masking tape
Diluted PVA glue
Fine sandpaper
White paint
Assortment of poster paints
Non-toxic clear gloss varnish

1 Take two double spread sheets of newspaper and twist them tightly to form a 'rope'. Tape the ends of the rope, and then bend it to form a fat rectangle about 15 cm (6 in) long, with one end extending about 5 cm (2 in). This end will form the dog's head. Firmly tape the rectangle to hold it in place.

2 Make the dog's limbs in the same way as the body and head. Using a single sheet of newspaper, form a thinner 'rope', and tape it along its length. Cut it into four pieces about 7–10 cm (3–4 in) long, and fix each one in place on the dog's body using masking tape. Add the dog's ears and tail with small, thin rolls of paper.

3 Soak newspaper strips in diluted PVA glue and cover the dog with three layers of papier-mâché strips. Leave it to dry overnight in a warm place.

4 Sand down the papier-mâché dog shape, and prime it with two coats of white paint. Decorate the dog with poster paints, and then seal with two coats of clear gloss varnish.

STAINED GLASS PENDANT

Hang this 'stained glass' pendant in your window and enjoy the bright colours as the light shines through. You could choose your own design from a plate or a piece of jewellery or you could base it on the Celtic ship used here.

YOU WILL NEED
Black cartridge paper
Craft knife
Coloured tissue paper
Glue
Ribbon

1 Trace and draw out your designs twice in black cartridge paper and then cut out the shapes with a sharp craft knife. Be careful to cut inside the lines so that the shape remains intact.

2 Select which colour tissue paper is to go where and then trace off and cut to shape. Start to glue your tissue paper on to the back of one of the black frames, using a separate piece to cover each area. You can use as many or as few colours as you wish. When you feel more confident you can start to shade your picture by putting one layer of paper over another, giving a darker tone.

3 When all the shapes have been filled, glue and fix the other black frame on to the back to neaten. Attach a ribbon to the top and display in your window.

■ ABSTRACT STAINED GLASS

This is a very effective but easy way to make an abstract piece of 'stained glass' work, which is great fun to do and because the pieces are torn it is always slightly unpredictable.

YOU WILL NEED
Two sheets of black paper
Coloured tissue paper
Glue

1 Cut out two
■ identical frames from the sheets of black paper. Take the coloured tissue papers and tear them into strips.

2 Cut out two
■ pieces of tissue paper just larger than the frame opening, one in a light colour and one in a darker colour. Glue the lighter one onto the back of one of the frames. Arrange the torn strips so that they overlap the edges of the lighter tissue paper, and glue them into place.

3 Finally, stick
■ down the darker piece of tissue paper, sandwiching the strips in place. Glue down the other black frame on top.

∎ V A S E

This vase is not waterproof, but it can be used to hold artificial or dried flowers, and is a very decorative 'objet d'art' in its own right. It is made using a simple basic method that can be easily adapted to make other shapes or sizes of vase.

YOU WILL NEED
Heavy corrugated cardboard
Strong clear glue
Masking tape
Newspaper
Diluted PVA glue
Fine sandpaper
White paint
Assorted poster paints
Non-toxic clear gloss varnish

Front/back

Cut 2

Wall of vase

1 Scale up the shapes from the template to the size required and transfer onto heavy corrugated cardboard and cut out. The vase wall should be placed on the cardboard so that the corrugations run vertically down the wall's width. This will make it easier to bend the wall into

shape. Glue and tape the wall into place right around the inside edge of one of the vase pieces. Cover the pieces with a coat of diluted PVA glue to help prevent warping, and let them dry for three to four hours in a warm place.

2 Next, tear narrow strips of newspaper and soak in diluted PVA glue. Cover the pieces of vase with four layers of papier-mâché strips. Leave to dry flat in a warm place overnight, and then smooth them lightly with fine sandpaper. Cover the inside of the vase and wall, and the remaining vase piece with two coats of white paint.

3 Join the vase together, with the painted surfaces to the inside. Glue the pieces together with strong clear glue and tape over the join with masking tape.

4 Leave the vase to dry for at least an hour. When dry seal its joined edge with three layers of papier-mâché strips, taking care to ensure a smooth surface by pushing out any small air bubbles or excess glue.

6 To decorate, lightly draw on the design with a pencil and then fill in using poster paints. When the paint is completely dry, apply a coat of clear gloss varnish.

5 Let the vase dry overnight, sand it lightly, and prime with two coats of white paint.

PERFORMING PIERROT

Children will love to watch the clever movements of this traditional Pierrot puppet. Why not make a couple and put on a show?

YOU WILL NEED
Blue, white and red paper
Black felt-tip pen
Glue
4 paper fasteners
Metal skewer or scissor blade
Curtain ring
Thin string

1 Scale up the pieces from the template to the size required and transfer to the coloured paper. Cut out the shapes for the clown: one body, two legs, two arms and a hat in blue, collar, cuffs and pom-poms in white. Mark on reference dots with a black pen. First make up the face by gluing on his hat and rosy cheeks. Draw the face details in with a black felt-tip pen.

2 Glue the pom-poms onto the hat, front and Pierrot's boots, and stick on the collar and cuffs.

3 Match up the dots on the body and limbs and join them all together by pushing the paper fasteners through both layers. Open out the fasteners on the back.

4 On the reverse side, pull the limbs downwards and pierce a hole at the top of each arm using a skewer or scissor blade. Thread a length of thin string through each hole and knot at both ends, on the reverse side. Repeat this with the legs to form two 'cross bars'.

5 Thread a long piece of string through a curtain ring. Attach one end to the centre of the arm string and the other end to the centre of the leg string. Trim where necessary. The strings should not be slack when the limbs are 'at rest'. When the strings are firmly fixed, pull the ring and watch Pierrot perform.

PICTURE CALENDAR

A simple idea that even children can make to give as presents. Calendar booklets are available from stationery shops.

YOU WILL NEED
Chosen picture
Card
Coloured paper
Glue
Calendar booklet
Matching ribbon
Sticky tape

1 Cut out a favourite picture from an old greetings card or a magazine.

2 Now cut out a larger piece of card and then choose a coloured paper which will match the colours in your picture. Glue the paper onto the card to cover.

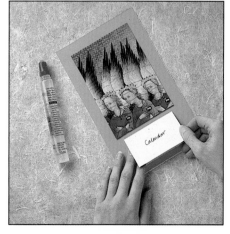

3 Position and glue the picture onto the card, making sure that it is centred, but leaving more space at the bottom in order to accommodate the calendar booklet. Glue the calendar in place. Make a loop at the top with some matching coloured ribbon, and fix it at the back with sticky tape. For an added detail, make a little bow from the same ribbon and glue it just above the booklet.

■ BANGLES AND BEADS

If you want some new accessories and to wear something that nobody else will have, this jewellery that is made from paper could be just what you are looking for.

YOU WILL NEED
Patterned paper
Contrasting coloured card
Pencil or paint brush
Glue
Bead thread
Sticky tape

1 To start, cut 30 cm (12 in) strips of marbled or decorated paper and taper them so that they measure 4 cm (1½ in) at the base and 1 cm (½ in) at the tip. Then cut a small length of contrasting coloured card, wrap it around a pencil or paint brush and fix it with glue.

2 Now apply some more glue to the length of the triangular strip and, beginning with the wider end, start to wrap around the card, so that the strip is kept central. Make several more of these beads, and thread them onto a length of bead thread to form a necklace.

3 To make a matching bangle, cut a long strip of white card and curl it round into a ring, large enough to slip over your hand. Fix by taping it.

4 Now cut long strips of your chosen decorated paper and after gluing them at one end, start to wind them one by one around the bangle shape.

CUT-OUT DOLLS

This charming couple are modern versions of the cut-out dolls that have been popular for several centuries. They have 'casual' and 'smart' outfits, so are ready for any occasion!

YOU WILL NEED
Thick white paper
Felt-tip pens or coloured pencils
Glue
Thin card
Craft knife

1 Start by scaling up the designs from the template to the size required. Next transfer them to white paper.

2 Colour in the dolls and their clothes with felt-tip pens or coloured pencils according to your own fashion scheme.

3 Stick the dolls onto the thin card. Cut carefully around the dolls and their clothes with scissors. Using a craft knife, lightly score the fold line of the stand at the bottom of each doll, making sure you do not cut right through. Fold along the scored line to make a prop to help the dolls stand upright. To dress the dolls, simply fold each white tab over to the back of the body.

CHINESE HAT

Celebrate Chinese New Year with a stylish Oriental hat. There is no fixed design to follow, so you can have fun adding your own characters.

YOU WILL NEED
Beige and white card
Black ink or paint
Double-sided tape

1 Cut a 48 cm (19 in) diameter circle out of beige card. Using black ink or paint, make up Chinese characters and decorate the beige card with them.

2 Now cut a line from the edge of the circle to the centre and overlap one edge over the other to give form to the hat. Stick in position with double-sided tape.

3 Take a strip of narrow card, long enough to go around your head, and tape the ends together to make a headband.

4 Fix the headband to the underneath of the Chinese hat with pieces of tape as illustrated.

POT-POURRI PUNNET

Bring the sweet smell of your favourite flowers into the room all year round with a basket of pot-pourri. Stir it occasionally to bring out the scent.

YOU WILL NEED
Small basket
Tissue paper
Needle
Silver thread
Pot-pourri

1 Take a small gift basket and line it with coloured tissue paper. A bright pink has been chosen here to bring out the colours of the pot-pourri.

2 Now take another piece of the same tissue paper and roll it up into a sausage shape and twist.

3 Take a needle and some silver thread. Oversew the twisted tissue paper around the top edge of the basket.

4 Fix the two ends of the sausage so that they overlap and secure them with a couple of stitches or a dab of glue. Now place the pot-pourri into the basket to give your room a lovely aroma as well as look attractive.

POPULAR POPPIES

The stark simplicity of bright red poppies with their black centres makes them an ideal flower to craft in paper.

YOU WILL NEED
Garden wire
Cotton wool (surgical cotton)
Green, black and red crêpe paper
Glue
Sticky tape

1 To make the stem cut a length of garden wire. Bend the top to make a loop and trap a small amount of cotton wool in the loop. Cover this in a cut-out circle of green crêpe paper. Secure by wrapping tape around.

2 Next cut three small circles of black crêpe paper. Fringe the outer edges and then poke the other end of the wire through the centre and slide up to the green bud.

3 Cut out five petal shapes in red crêpe paper and stretch the outer edge with your finger tips so that they frill.

4 Glue the petals one by one around the base of the centre.

5 Finally, cover the stem in green crêpe paper by winding a long strip around diagonally and securing it at the base with sticky tape.

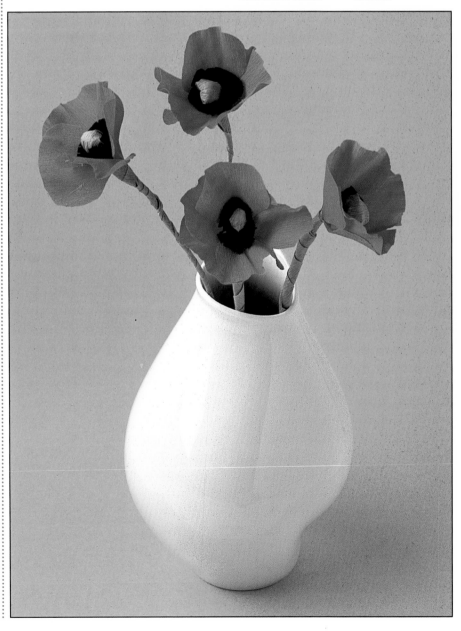

■ CHRISTMAS RING

This is a quick and easy way to make a
new collection of Christmas
decorations to hang on your tree
without spending a fortune. They are
made from wooden curtain rings,
covered in vivid crêpe paper.

YOU WILL NEED
Crêpe paper
Wooden curtain rings
Glue
Thin ribbon

1 Cut 2 cm (¾ in)
wide strips of
coloured crêpe
paper. Take a
wooden curtain ring
and wind the strips
of crêpe paper
around the ring to
cover. Glue ends in
place.

2 Now take a thin
ribbon and secure
it at the top of the
ring. As before, wind
it around the ring
leaving gaps to
reveal the paper.
When you have
worked the ribbon
back to the top,
secure it and then
make a loop for
hanging.

3 To finish off,
make a bow out
of the crêpe paper
and stick it on at the
top of the ring.

CHRISTMAS TREE BOWS

Dress up your tree with shimmering bows for a glamorous film-star style Christmas. Match bows to baubles for a co-ordinated look.

YOU WILL NEED
Metallic corrugated paper
Stapler
Metallic tissue paper
Double-sided tape
Ribbon

1 From the metallic corrugated paper cut out an oblong measuring 18 × 12 cm (7 × 4½ in).

Gather in the centre to make the bow shape and staple in position.

2 Now take a length of metallic tissue paper and wrap it around the centre of the bow to cover the staples. However do not

wrap the whole length around but leave some excess to fall at the front. Fix at the back with double-sided tape.

3 Now cut two rectangles for the tails in the metallic paper measuring 20

× 8 cm (8 × 3 in). Cut darts at one end of each tail.

4 Make one pleat at the top of the tails. Staple each

pleat and then staple the tails together.

5 Now attach the tails to the back of the bow with double-sided tape. Make a loop with a

piece of ribbon and stick it to the back of the finished bow for hanging.

SOAP-BOX

Guest soaps come in all shapes and colours. Decorate a box in pretty shades to match your soaps for an attractive present.

YOU WILL NEED
Empty circular box
Assorted coloured card
Glue
Tissue paper
Soaps

1 Cover the outside of the box by gluing a strip of coloured card around the side.

2 This particular gift uses shell-shaped soaps, so draw shell shapes onto coloured cards that complement the colours of the soaps.

3 Cut out the shell shapes and stick them onto the outside of the box.

4 Scrunch up a large piece of tissue paper and arrange it inside the box. Place the soaps on top of the tissue paper.

BOWLED OVER

This bowl is made by a traditional method where layers of papier-mâché are laid into a greased mould and removed when dry. For this project, an ordinary china bowl has been used, but all sorts of items can make interesting moulds – just remember to grease them first, otherwise they will be permanently lined with paper!

YOU WILL NEED
Bowl suitable for using as a mould
Petroleum jelly
Newspaper
Diluted PVA glue
Heavy corrugated card
Strong clear glue
Masking tape
Fine sandpaper
White paint
Assortment of poster paints
Non-toxic clear gloss varnish

1 Coat the inside of the bowl with five layers of PVA-soaked newspaper strips, allowing for an overlap of 2½ cm (1 in). Leave to dry in a warm place for 48 hours.

2 Gently prise the paper bowl from its mould with a blunt knife, and leave it upside down to dry for a few hours.

3 Trim the ragged edge to about ½ cm (¼ in).

4 Cut a zigzag bowl rim from the thick cardboard and lay it on the top of the papier-mâché bowl rim. Stick the rim on the bowl with strong clear glue, and hold it in place with masking tape. Allow the glue to dry for an hour or so and then paper over the rim, covering the joins carefully.

5 Paper the underside of the rim in the same way. Leave the bowl to dry for 24 hours. Lightly sand down the surface of the bowl, and then prime it with two coats of white paint.

6 Draw in any decoration with pencil first, and then decorate the bowl with poster paints. Let the bowl dry thoroughly, and then seal it with two coats of clear gloss varnish.

TAKE A LETTER

As well as paper and card, this letter rack also requires a block of wood to give it a firm base. Cover it in patterned paper to match your desk accessories.

YOU WILL NEED

Block of wood $19\frac{1}{2} \times 4\frac{1}{2} \times 2$ cm
  ($7\frac{1}{2} \times 1\frac{3}{4} \times \frac{3}{4}$ in)
Patterned paper
Glue or waterbased wood adhesive
Mounting card

1 Entirely cover the block of wood in the patterned paper and glue in place. Trim it where necessary.

2 Cut three pieces of mounting card, one piece measuring 25 × 13 cm (10 × 5 in) and the other two measuring 20 × 9 cm (8 × 3½ in). With each bit of card, measure and cut out a piece of paper slightly larger than the card itself. Glue the paper onto the card, and mitre the corners carefully by snipping off the corners diagonally and folding the turnings on to the back, making sure that they are well stuck down. Repeat with each piece of card.

3 Now stick a piece of paper slightly smaller than the card onto the back.

4 Using a strong glue or waterbased wood adhesive stick the smaller, front card to the narrow edge of the covered piece of wood, making sure it is centred. Glue the back card in the same way.

5 To complete the letter rack, position and glue it onto the covered base.

PAPER PROJECTS

ADVENT CALENDAR

Make the countdown to Christmas even more exciting with this beautiful tree advent calendar. The windows are decorated with pictures cut out from old Christmas cards.

YOU WILL NEED
Red, green and orange card
Thin cardboard
Craft knife
Old greetings cards
Glue
Silver metallic pen

1 Cut out two tree shapes, one in red card and the other in green. Use a 2 cm (¾ in) square template of thin cardboard to mark out 25 windows at random on the green tree. Now cut along three sides of each window with a craft knife.

2 Place the green tree onto the red tree so that it is slightly higher and gives the green tree a red line on the bottom edges.

Carefully open each window and mark their position on the red tree in pencil. Remove the green tree. Cut out 25 small pictures from old Christmas cards and glue them onto the pencilled squares on the red Christmas tree.

3 Now glue the green tree onto the red one making sure that all the windows line up.

4 Decorate the tree with cut-out circles of red and orange card to suggest the Christmas tree baubles.

5 Using a silver pen draw a bow above each bauble and then number the windows 1 to 25.

■ WASTE PAPER BOX

Waste paper boxes can make elegant gifts that can be put to use straight away. They can be covered in paper that matches the decor of the room they are intended for, or else in paper of your favourite design.

YOU WILL NEED
Thick card
Dark contrasting or toning paper
Impact adhesive
Decorative paper

1 For this waste paper box, cut out one square in thick card measuring 20 cm (9 in). Now measure and cut out from the same type of card the four sides so that they are 20 cm (9 in) wide, with a height of 25 cm (11 in). Cover one side of all these pieces with a dark toning paper.

2 Next glue the sides onto the base and to each other using an impact adhesive.

3 Now cut out a square of decorative paper measuring 24 cm (10 in). Firmly glue it onto the base and cut the corners diagonally. Glue the turnings around and up onto the sides of the container to give the box extra strength.

4 To cover, cut a piece of the decorative paper large enough to go around the whole of the box. Stick it on and trim where necessary at the base to create a neat finish.

5 At the top, turn the excess paper over and glue down onto the inside of the box, after mitring the corners. This will produce a very professional look.

■ DOLL

This doll is formed from tightly taped and compacted newspaper twists. The resulting structure is very sturdy and quite large dolls or other toys could be constructed using this method.

YOU WILL NEED
Newspaper
Masking tape
Diluted PVA glue
Fine sandpaper
White paint
Selection of poster paints
Black ink (optional)
Non-toxic clear gloss varnish

1 First, twist a double sheet of newspaper together to form a 'rope' and tape the top, about 5 cm (2 in) down, to form the doll's head. Cut the remaining paper 'rope' to the desired length to form the body, and secure it with masking tape.

2 Cover the body and head with strips of masking tape to add extra strength. Next, make the arms and legs by the same process, twisting smaller pieces of paper and taping them along their length. Cut the resulting 'ropes' to the right length, and tape them firmly in place on the doll's body.

3 Tear some newspaper into thin strips and soak in diluted PVA glue. Then cover the doll with four layers of papier-mâché. To make the doll's hair, hands and feet, roll up small strips of glue-soaked paper between finger and thumb to form pellets of pulp and stick them in place on the head. Paper over the pulp hair with short, thin strips of paper.

4 Let the doll dry overnight in a warm place. When completely dry, lightly smooth the surface with fine sandpaper and prime it with two coats of white paint.

5 When the paint has dried thoroughly, draw in the features of the doll with pencil and fill in the design with poster paints. Define the decoration with black ink if more detail is needed. Seal the doll with two coats of non-toxic clear gloss varnish and allow to dry.

DESIGNER PENCIL POT

This pencil pot is a lovely idea to cheer up your own desk, or it can make a beautiful personalized gift for a friend. The matching pencils add an artistic touch.

YOU WILL NEED
Empty cardboard tube or salt
*   container*
Patterned paper
Glue
Pencils

1 First of all you will need to cover the inside of the container. Measure the height and circumference of the pot and cut out two pieces of paper, slightly larger. You could use wallpaper, wrapping paper or marbled paper.

2 Take one of the pieces, glue it and carefully slot it into the inside of the pot, pressing it around the inside walls.

3 Cut darts on the excess paper at the top and glue them down to the outside one by one.

4 Take the other piece of paper and stick it to the outside so that the edge is flush with the top of the pot.

5 Once again cut darts into the excess length at the bottom and glue them onto the base.

6 Now draw around the base of the pot onto the patterned paper and cut out a circle slightly smaller. Glue this and drop it inside the bottom.

7 Cut out another circle and glue it to the outside base.

8 To make the matching pencils, cut out a strip of the same patterned paper the length of the pencils and approximately twice the width. Glue it and place the pencil at one edge and roll. Trim the paper where necessary.

DESK BLOTTER

To make the blotter special it is a good idea to select a wrapping paper to suit the type of desk area. You could choose a hand-made marbled paper for a very traditional look, or an abstract paper or two co-ordinating plain papers for a more modern effect.

YOU WILL NEED
Thick card
Patterned paper
Glue
Thin card
Coloured paper
Blotting paper

1 Cut a piece of thick card 46 × 30 cm (18 × 12 in). This will be the finished size of the blotter. Cut your chosen paper 3 cm (1 in) larger all around than the card.

2 Next fold and glue the edges onto the back of the card, mitring the corners by trimming them diagonally.

3 For the corner pieces cut four triangles in thin card measuring 10 × 10 × 14 cm (4 × 4 × 5½ in) and cover them in coloured paper cut to the same size first. Glue and turn down the bottom edge and the top point. Repeat this for all four corner pieces.

4 Position the corner pieces onto the corners of the blotter. Turn the board over and fold the edges around, gluing them securely.

5 Cut another piece of coloured paper the same size as the blotter and glue it on to the back. Trim where necessary.

6 Insert a piece of blotting paper under the corners.

CUT-OUT
ANIMALS

The chicken, frog, and elephant are
held together with paper fasteners and
have moveable limbs. They are very
simple in construction, and many other
animals could be attempted using the
same process.

YOU WILL NEED
Heavy paper or thin card
Felt-tip pens or coloured pencils
Craft knife
Paper fasteners
Glue

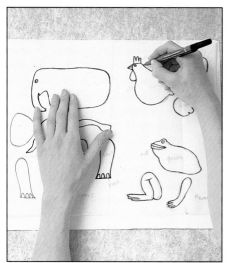

1 Scale up your
chosen animal
from the template to
the required size,
and transfer the
pieces to paper or
card. Cut two bodies
for each animal.
Remember that one
will have to be cut *in
reverse* so that the
bodies can be stuck
together. Next, cut
two of each leg,
wing, ear and so on.
To transfer the
pattern in reverse,
simply turn it over.

2 Next, colour each
piece of animal
with felt-tip pen or
coloured pencils,
and cut them all out,
keeping the parts
separate.

3 To fix the animal
together, make a
small incision with a
craft knife at the
limb positions in
each body, and at
the top of each body
part. Push a paper
fastener through the
front of each body
part, through the
body, and open it
out on the other side
to secure the animal.

4 To join the two
halves together,
spread a little glue
along the top edge
of one half of the
animal's body, and
stick it to the other.

INDEX

A

Abstract pop-up, 66
Abstract stationery, 26
Advent calendar, 121
Animals, cut-out, 127
Antique marbling, 73

B

Bag, locking, 84
Baroque baubles, 12
Batik effects, 25
Baubles, baroque, 12
Binding, beautiful, 80
Block printing, 40
Booklet card, 31
Books
    beautiful binding, 80
Bow-tie gift wrap, 69
Bowl
    bowled over, 118
Boxes
    chocolate box, 92
    Christmas tree gift box, 97
    curvy-sided, 29
    desk tidy, 72
    gift box, 15
    lidded, 53
    one-piece gift boxes, 74
    soap-box, 117
    straight-sided, 24
    waste paper, 122
Brown paper stationery, 77

C

Calendars
    Advent, 121
    picture, 108
Candy cones, 54
Cards
    across the border, 56
    centre-opening, 38
    flower power, 78
    sculptured tops, 86
    tearing hurry, 71
    to my Valentine, 38
    Valentine's heart, 75
    21st birthday pop-up, 43
Chinese hat, 112
Chocolate box, 92
Christmas gift tags, 50
Christmas ring, 115
Christmas tree
    bows, 116
    gift box, 97
    3-D, 65
Classic lines, 16
Collage tags, 44
Concentric twist, 64
Cone hats, 48
Cracker wrapping, 20
Curvy-sided box, 29
Cut-and-thread paper, 39
Cut-out animals, 127
Cut-out dolls, 110
Cut-out stationery, 70

D

Decorative doily, 47
Decorative sponging, 36
Decorative wallet, 42
Desk tidy, 72
Doily, decorative, 47
Doll, 123
    cut-out, 110

E

Easter Egg basket, 91
Envelopes
    elegant, 19
    envelope letters, 87
    practical, 67

F

Fan, oriental, 13
Flowers
    popular poppies, 114
Frames
    framed piece, 95

G

Gift bag, 58
Gift box, 15
Gift tags
    booklet card, 31
    Christmas, 50
    collage, 44
    fruit 'n' veg, 79
    marbled, 82
    secret messages, 51
    tag time, 23
Giftwrap
    bow-tie gift wrap, 69
    it's a cracker, 20
    paint and paper, 17
    secret messages, 51
    sphere, wrapping, 45
    two-tone, 11

H

Hats
    Chinese, 112
    cone, 48
    pirates ahoy, 96

J

Jewellery
    bangles and beads, 109
    ring and bangle, 93

L

Letter rack, 120
Lidded box, 53
Locking bag, 84

M

Masks
    king, 100
    tiger, tiger, 90

N

Name cards
    Egyptian evening, 76
    places on a theme, 46
    places please, 61
    stand-up place names, 83
Napkin holders
    this little piggy, 32
Napkin rings
    Egyptian evening, 76
    ring the changes, 68
Napkins
    natty, 10
    spot-on, 57
    well-dressed, 14
Notelet holder, 62

O

One-piece gift boxes, 74
Oriental fan, 13

P

Paint
    combing and feathering, 52
    decorative sponging, 52
Paper-making, 34
Papier-mâché
    puppet, 98
    spotty dog, 101
Pencil pot, designer, 124
Picture calendar, 108
Place cards See Name cards
Place mats
    Egyptian evening, 76
    twelfth knight, 18
Place settings
    this little piggy, 32
Plaque, 94
Poppies, popular, 114
Pot pourri punnet, 113
Printing, block, 40
Puppets
    papier-mâché, 98
    performing Pierrot, 106

Q

Quills and coils, 30

R

Ribbon
    rosettes, 37
    plaits and curls, 22

S

Sculpture
    abstract pop-up, 66
    concentric twist, 64
Soap-box, 117
Speckling effects, 28
Sphere, wrapping, 45
Sponging, decorative, 36
Spot-on napkins, 57
Spotty dog, 101
Stained glass
    abstract, 103
    pendant, 102
Stationery
    abstract, 26
    brown paper, 77
    cut-and-thread paper, 39
    cut-out, 70
    envelope letters, 87
    hopping frogs, 33
    notelet holder, 62
    practical envelopes, 67
    stencil style, 60
    tiger stripes, 33
Stencil style writing paper, 60
Stencilling, 21
Straight-sided box, 24

T

Tiger, tiger, 90
Twelfth knight, 18
Two-tone giftwrap, 11

V

Valentine card, 38
Valentine's heart, 75
Vase, 104

W

Wallet, decorative, 42
Waste paper box, 122
Well-dressed napkins, 14
Wrapping paper,
    bow-tie gift wrap, 69
    brown paper stationery, 77
    classic lines, 16
    cut-and-thread paper, 39
    cut-out stationery, 70
    envelope letters, 87
    hopping frogs, 33
    notelet holder, 62
    paint and paper, 17
    sphere, wrapping, 45
    stencil style, 60
    tiger stripes, 33
    two-tone, 11

21st birthday pop-up, 43
3-D Christmas tree, 65